Dishing It Out

IN THE SERIES

WOMEN IN THE POLITICAL ECONOMY

EDITED BY RONNIE J. STEINBERG

Dishing It Out

Power and Resistance among Waitresses in a New Jersey Restaurant

Greta Foff Paules

TEMPLE UNIVERSITY PRESS

PHILADELPHIA

Temple University Press, Philadelphia 19122
Copyright © 1991 by Temple University. All rights reserved
Published 1991
Printed in the United States of America

The paper used in this publication meets the minimum
requirements of American National Standard for Information
Sciences—Permanence of Paper for Printed Library Materials,
ANSI Z39.48-1984 ⊚

Library of Congress Cataloging-in-Publication Data

Paules, Greta Foff.
    Dishing it out : power and resistance among waitresses in a
New Jersey restaurant / Greta Foff Paules.
    p.   cm. — (Women in the political economy)
    Includes bibliographical references (p. 207).
    ISBN 0-87722-887-6 (alk. paper) — ISBN 0-87722-888-4
(pbk. : alk. paper)
    1. Waitresses—New Jersey—Case studies.   2. Restaurants,
lunch rooms, etc.—New Jersey—Management—Case
studies.   I. Title.   II. Series.
TX925.P38   1991
305.43'642—dc20   91-10999
                                                  CIP

*To my husband
and in memory of my mother and father*

Contents

Acknowledgments   *ix*

1. Introduction   1

2. "Getting" and "Making" a Tip   23

3. The Limits of Managerial Authority   49

4. Sources of Autonomy   77

5. Up a Crooked Ladder   105

6. Resisting the Symbolism of Service   131

7. Conclusion   167

   Notes   *189*

   References   *207*

   Index   *219*

Acknowledgments

Financial support for this research was provided by Princeton University (graduate fellowship) and a Grant-in-Aid of Research from Sigma Xi, The Scientific Research Society. Both are gratefully acknowledged.

Portions of this work have appeared previously in *Cross-Cultural Management and Organizational Culture,* Tomoko Hamada and Ann Jordan, eds. (Paules 1990b).

I am indebted to Professor Kay Warren for her guidance, support, and inspiration throughout the writing of the dissertation upon which this work is based. I am deeply grateful to Professor Rena Lederman for her thoughtful suggestions on an earlier draft and for saying the right thing at the right time; to Ronnie Steinberg and Michael Ames for their valuable suggestions for later revisions; to Professor Hildred Geertz for her guidance and kindness from an early stage of my graduate career; to Professor Lawrence Rosen for his helpful comments on the initial proposal for this research; and to Professor Susan Gal for her support and sensitivity at a critical time, and for reminding me to remember language. I express warm thanks to Professor Pam Crabtree and to

Acknowledgments

Carol Zanca for their friendship, good will, and good advice, and to Pam also, for showing me another side of anthropology; to Pauline Caulk for always knowing the answer; and to Krishen Kak, who gave me the majority of newspaper and magazine articles cited in this text, and fed the cats to boot.

The contribution of my brilliant and talented mother to my education can never be justly acknowledged.

My husband's unrelenting industry and fortitude have provided me with a worthy model over the past five years. He put up with more than he should have, and apologized when he should not have. He supported me when my last days were his last days. For all these things, I thank and love him.

My warmest gratitude goes to my sisters for their confidence and for caring if I came back, to the Pauleses III for their kindness and encouragement, and to Harry for showing me it could be done.

Final thanks go to my informants at Route for their time, honesty, and insight. Special appreciation is due to Ken, Kim, Nera, Nancy, Celina, and most of all to Mae, who made me laugh.

Dishing It Out

I

Introduction

On the whole, [women] accept what is. One of their distinguishing traits is resignation. . . . Women feel they are powerless against things. . . . "Women are born to suffer," they say; "it's life—nothing can be done about it."
—*Simone de Beauvoir*, "The Existential Paralysis of Women"

I don't take any nonsense from no one. . . . I don't take no junk . . . because I demand to make sure that I treat you fair, you treat me fair. . . . So . . . I told him [a customer], I said, "Don't you dare talk to me this way, cause I take this pot of water and I throw it right into your damn face."
—*Route waitress*

    This is a study of a small group of women who wait tables in a family-style restaurant in New Jersey. It is a study of women who are neither organized nor upwardly mobile yet actively and effectively strive to protect and enhance their position at work. It is about women who refuse to submit unquestioningly to the dictates of management, to absorb the abuses of a hurried and often hostile public, or to internalize a negative image of self promoted by the symbols of servitude, which pervade their work. It is about women who "don't take no junk."

Route Restaurant

The restaurant where this study was conducted, referred to here as Route, or Kendelport Route, is located on a busy interstate highway in an area undergoing rapid residential and commercial development.[1] It is surrounded by malls, business parks, research campuses, and housing complexes in various stages of completion. Great expanses of bulldozed forest and billboards announcing forthcoming construction portend continued development in years to come. The entire region, however, suffers from an intense shortage of labor that may temper its growth in the future. Help-wanted signs promising an enjoyable working environment, flexible hours, and good pay and benefits adorn the front windows and doors of many stores and restaurants. Some signs, including the one that hangs on the door at Route, are never removed. This climate of desperation has far-reaching implications for employer–employee relations and for the quality of work life within the restaurant.

Route belongs to a well-known restaurant chain, which developed from a donut stand founded in the early fifties. The chain has more than twelve hundred units or "stores" located throughout the United States and several abroad. The caliber of the chain's food, service, and decor places it in the mid to lower range of the restaurant spectrum. Bon vivant urban professionals do not condescend to dine at Route, which is not greasy enough to be camp. The restaurant does appeal to budget-conscious families, senior citizens on fixed incomes, athletic teams, and church groups. In the predawn hours, Route absorbs the night life that has been dispelled from nearby bars at closing, as well as teenagers who congregate in packs over coffee and fries, and drug dealers who ostentatiously stack fifty- and hundred-dollar bills on booth tables, then stiff their waitresses. Like many roadside restaurants, Route is also the occasional resting place of the homeless, who find refuge on a stool at the counter from the cold, the heat, and the loneliness outside.

Route waitresses include teenagers and women in their sixties; mothers-to-be (three waitresses were pregnant when the research ended), teen-mothers, grandmothers, and women with no children; full-time workers who have been waiting tables for decades, and women who also hold jobs as telephone operators, cleaning women, cashiers, or companions for the ill. There is a Route waitress who picked cotton and peanuts alongside sharecropper parents when she was six and wore bleached flour sacks for slips, and another whose father is rumored by her co-workers to own "a big, fine mansion . . . with a maid and everything. . . . A girl who was brought up with nannies." In contrast to some restaurants in the area, Route attracts few college students to its waitressing staff. This may be due to the intensely serious work atmosphere or to the stigma attached to Route waitresses. A sense of how the public perceives the restaurant was suggested by a comedian on the "Tonight Show," who hypothesized that Route purposefully hired the ugliest women it could find in order to make the food appear more appetizing.

Approximately thirty waitresses work at Kendelport Route. One to eight waitresses may be on the floor at a given time.[2] The restaurant employs dishwashers or "service assistants," who are often referred to as busboys though they do not bus tables, which is the waitress's job. It employs cooks and prep cooks, and on busy shifts hostesses are scheduled to work the register and seat incoming parties. The managerial staff consists of two managers and a general manager. There are also *PICs* and *SCs* (persons-in-charge and service coordinators): employees, usually waitresses, who act as managers for one or two nights a week, allowing regular managers an occasional night off. Because there are no regular persons-in-charge or service coordinators, *PIC* or *SC* is generally understood as something one does, not is. This is reflected in the language of the restaurant: a waitress is rarely referred to as a *PIC* or *SC;* rather she is said to be *PICing* or *SCing.*

There are three shifts at Route: day, swing, and grave, or graveyard. Day is staffed primarily by full-time workers who have been with the restaurant a long time. It is the most prestigious shift, because it is the fastest, busiest, and most lucrative. It is also the most competitive. Day waitresses, one employee remarked, "[are] here to fight tooth and nail for customers, to make money, to get as many parties as they want to, to fight over what station they're in, . . . to fight over who gets the next party." Other shifts admire day waitresses for their skill and resent them for their aggressiveness.

Swing, the evening shift, is "more laid-back" than day. It is staffed by part- and full-time workers, many of whom work day or grave part of the week, or have worked other shifts in the past. There is considerable movement of waitresses in and out of this shift, and workers tend to be younger, though not always less experienced than day waitresses. Because dinner is the main meal served on swing, customer checks are higher and turnover slower than on day shift.[3] The slow turnover and overall decrease in customer volume at night counterbalance the increase in individual check size with the result that swing waitresses usually do not make as much in tips as day workers.

4

Introduction

Graveyard is "a whole strung-out ball game . . . a joke . . . a circus and treated as such." Grave servers are the youngest and least experienced in the restaurant. They enjoy the greatest latitude in the conduct of their work and violate company policy most often and flagrantly. This is partly because there is no manager on duty for part of this shift, but also because few employees are willing to work graveyard and management is constrained to disregard the misdoings of those who are. Tips on grave are poor and there is a high incidence of stiffing and walkouts.[4] As compensation, grave waitresses receive slightly higher wages than servers on other shifts. Occasionally grave workers receive preposterously large tips from customers who are intoxicated, high, or stimulated to recklessness by the boisterous late-night atmosphere. In one instance, a waitress reportedly received a forty-dollar tip on a sixty-dollar check.

Customers on grave are frequently rowdy, drunk, and unmanageable, and it is not uncommon for the police to be called in to break up fights. The following incident, recounted by a grave waitress, is typical:

> Kerrie used to work Saturday night graveyard. . . . [One night she] ended up spilling a little bit of milk as she was going to put it on the table, cause the guy backed up his seat; so he took the water and threw it at her all over and said, "How dare you throw anything on me? And blah, blah, blah, blah, blah." And Kerrie proceeded to grab a glass of water, whoosh, [and said], "Don't you dare do that to me." . . . And [the fight] broke out from there, where he cornered Kerrie, screaming at her face and punching the wall around her. So then I grabbed a hold of the back of *him,* pulled him off, and then [the

manager was] running around . . . doing abso-
lutely nothing.

The restaurant recently hired security guards to maintain
order on weekend nights, but it remains a rough shift.
One waitress commented:

> You have to have a certain personality to work
> graveyard. . . . You have to have that tough. . . .
> I'm not a tough person, I'm very soft, . . . but I
> put up my little barricade of tough. I won't take
> no shit from nobody.

Grave workers are admired for their toughness and crit-
icized for their laziness, unreliability, and lack of disci-
pline. Grave is the least prestigious shift in the restaurant.

Job categories at Route are segregated along gen-
der lines. During the research period, all managers at
Kendelport Route were male, but there were female
managers at other units in the district, and women had
managed at Kendelport in the past. All but one to two
cooks and dishwashers were male. By contrast, virtually
all servers were women. Of the few waiters who worked
at the restaurant, two were dating waitresses. One, a
rugged college student, reported being addressed as
"waitress" by inattentive customers: an indication that
the public is not accustomed to seeing waiters at Route.
Hostesses also tended to be women.[5]

The Work of the Waitress

In many respects, the waitress epitomizes the
position of women in low-reward, traditionally female

Introduction

occupations. Her work is rated among "the least skilled lower-class occupations" (Montagna 1977:372) and falls at the bottom of the occupational prestige hierarchy, ranking below butcher, coal miner, file clerk, telephone operator, and delivery truck driver (Rothman 1987:216). Waitresses would have a still lower prestige rating if they were evaluated independently of waiters, who predominate in higher-status restaurants. Waitressing wages are low: at the onset of this study servers at Route started at $1.71 an hour, 64 cents below minimum wage, and even those who have worked at the restaurant five or more years earn well under three dollars. Working conditions at Route are poor. In summer flies swarm in the waitresses' stations, where overflowing garbage bins emit a stench that has evoked complaints from more than one customer.[6] A single paper- and cigarette-strewn toilet serves the entire female staff, and the employee break room consists of a closet from which the door has been removed, presumably to permit the storage of broken chairs within. The break-room walls are papered with catsup-splattered memos on new menu items and worker safety; the ledge that serves as the employee dining table is piled with dirty plates and traversed by a variety of insect life. To the outsider or newcomer such accommodations are a depressing prospect, but the quality of restroom and break room is of little concern to the seasoned waitress, who rarely has time to use the bathroom and seldom takes formal breaks.

The waitress's work is physically and emotionally exhausting. Sudden surges in business or *rushes*, coupled with a high rate of absenteeism among her co-waitresses, mean that she is often compelled to wait on twice or three times the number of customers served under optimal conditions. She must maintain control over the resulting confusion of orders and reorders, spe-

7

cial requests, and complaints, remembering that the man at table six wants margarine not butter on his blueberry muffin, which he wants grilled not microwaved; the woman in eight wants her orange juice in a milk glass and skim milk for her tea; the boy in seven is still waiting for his omelette to come back without the cheese, and his sister is still waiting for a pencil to connect the dots on the children's menu. She must find quick solutions to the seemingly endless complications that arise in the course of each shift: the entrees for table two are up but the appetizers have yet to materialize;[7] the new waiter has served her customer's well-done New York steak to his party at the adjoining table; table five wants four orders of vegetable soup but there are only enough bowls for three, enough soup servings for two; and the to-go order is up, but the to-go containers are in the stockroom under a box she cannot lift on a shelf she cannot reach.

While she is struggling to keep order in her station, the waitress is called upon to answer phones, tend the register, process credit cards, seat customers, bus, wipe, and set her tables, scraping all plates and separating glasses and utensils into the appropriate bins. On busy days she may remain on her feet well over eight hours. At the end of her shift, she faces a daily stint of paper work and a list of stocking and cleaning tasks or *sidework*, which may include mixing vats of salad dressing, washing and chopping mountains of mushrooms, cleaning the hot fudge and syrup dispensers, and excavating the counters and floor of the waitresses' station from the wreckage of dirty dishes, broken glasses, and discarded food, which has accumulated during the rush.

Yet the physical tasks of waitressing are less exacting than the emotional challenges. Along with the duties of serving, the waitress has inherited from the nineteenth-century domestic a constellation of symbols

8

and a code of interaction that proclaim her subordination to her customers and assault her self-esteem on all fronts. She is directed to wear a uniform that recalls the housemaid's dress and is prohibited from eating, drinking, and resting in public view. She is constrained to address as *sir* or *ma'am* those who are in turn encouraged to address her by first name, and she is placed in the symbolically demeaning position of receiving the greater part of her income in the form of tips conferred as gifts by strangers. In all branches of the media, she and other service workers, like household domestics before them, are portrayed as ignorant, incompetent, apathetic, lazy, and slow. Apart from the damage that negative stereotyping can inflict on the waitress's sense of self-worth, it heightens the tension between server and served, predisposing the public to expect the worst from anyone on the employee side of a service counter. In addition, customers may be prompted by the symbolic scenery of service to adopt the posture of master toward servant, disregarding conventions of polite conduct when dealing with the waitress and freely venting their anger when complications arise in the course of their encounter.

Strategies of Action

At first glance it might appear that the Route waitress passively submits to the hardships of her work. She makes no attempt to improve her position through collective action, following a pattern increasingly typical of the food service industry.[8] Only 8 percent of workers employed in table-service restaurants are unionized (Bernard Grogan, pers. com. 1990), and union membership is declining. The Hotel Employees and Restaurant Employees' International Union (AFL-CIO), the principal union for waiters and waitresses (U.S. Department of Labor, Bureau of Labor Statistics 1986), reported a membership of 340,000 for 1983. By 1987 membership had dropped to 293,000 (Gifford 1988).[9] Nor does the Route waitress seek to improve her position by ascending the occupational ladder. On the contrary, she rejects opportunities to advance to the managerial ranks, in some instances choosing to return to the level of wage worker after occupying a managerial post in the past.

But the Route waitress is not passive. She is engaged in ongoing efforts to shield herself from the emotional and financial hazards of her occupation and advance her work interests. Her strategies of action include ways of speaking about and perceiving herself, her customers, and her work that subvert the restaurant's symbolism of servitude; methods of manipulating management to ensure her grievances and demands will be heeded; and techniques for controlling the movement of customers through the restaurant to maximize her tip income. These strategies of action belong to what James Scott (1985) refers to as the "garden" or everyday variety, not only because they are not especially dramatic (though a waitress throwing her order book and storming out the door at the height of a rush has an element of drama), but because they are "informal, often covert, and concerned largely with immediate, de facto gains" (Scott 1985:33)—confiscating an incoming party, deflecting attempted disparagement from a customer, avoiding performance of time-consuming and unprofitable tasks. Further, in contrast to organized, collective action, the waitress's methods of self-protection may be unconsciously implemented. This applies especially to strategies of self-perception and the linguistic conventions through which they are enacted and affirmed.

All waitresses are not equally skilled or aggressive in defending their interests. Full-time workers are more prone to rebuke impatient or impolite customers, more fearless in reproaching management, and more adept at manipulating the tipping system. But the distinction between full- and part-time employees is not easily drawn. A waitress who works one night a week may have worked forty hours in the past and may retain the skills and defiant attitude developed through her earlier experience. Rookies, full- or part-time, are more submissive to customers and managers than are experienced waitresses. They are also more sensitive to the abrasive atmosphere of the restaurant. One waitress remembered:

> When I first started, I cried. The cooks made me cry, the customers made me cry, my manager made me cry. I cried. I always cried.

Another waitress commented:

> I used to come home from work, when I first started . . . and go into my room and just cry. I'd be like, "God, I hate this place." But I'd come back and I'd come back and I'd come back and then you know you don't take things as bad.

Another waitress recalled her introduction to Route and how she has changed:

> When I first got there, little meek and mild me? So happy to get a job? I got threatened by [a manager] that if I didn't straighten up my act he was going to fire me . . . [because a rumor] went around the store that me and [another manager] got it on in the stockroom. . . . That left me in tears for a good two weeks. Now I'm saying, from

when I first came here, from being in tears over
something like that, to now where it's, "Touch
me, sucker, and I'll punch you in the mouth."

As she becomes acclimated to the tensions of her
work, the waitress's perception of the public changes.
"After you been working with the public for X amount of
years, you start seeing the good and the bad in people,
and the bad outweighs the good." With time she comes to
see impatience and hostility as an inherent characteristic
of her customers, not something she provokes by failing
to attend adequately to their needs. She adopts a de-
tached, calculating attitude toward her parties, viewing
them foremost in terms of their tipping potential.

You have the bums and the drunks coming in on
graveyard shift, and you have to deal with that.
You have to deal with their obscenity, their violence. . . . *But* they're good tippers though.

She becomes less tolerant of rudeness, advising a discour-
teous customer, "I think you better learn to tone that
voice of yours down. Cause you don't talk to me or nobody else like that." She refuses to wait on drug dealers
who have stiffed her in the past, calmly informing them,
"I'm not going to wait on you. You got all that money, you
sell all that crack on the streets, and you come here and
you can't even leave me a couple bucks?" One waitress
allegedly ran outside and jumped on the departing car of
a party that had left without paying its bill and presumably without leaving a tip.
      The strategies the experienced waitress employs
to improve her position at work are shaped to a large
extent by features of the restaurant industry that are not
found, or not in the same degree, in other occupations.

Among these features may be counted the tipping system, the chaotic work environment, chronic shortages of crucial supplies, the labor shortage, and the manager's role as fill-in man. In examining the relationship between the distinctive structure of the restaurant industry and the waitress's strategies of action, we will be reminded of the diversity of work environments in postindustrial society, and alerted to the dangers of applying issues and frameworks of analysis drawn from one sector of the work force to the problems and behavior of workers in another. Questions about the mobility patterns of employees, for instance, may not translate well across industries. To investigate barriers to occupational mobility among women makes sense in corporate environments where benefits, prestige, and autonomy are predicated on advancement. As we shall see, however, supervisory positions in the restaurant have been downgraded to the extent that managerial posts no longer represent a clear improvement over wage work. Indeed, it is probably more appropriate to question the motivations of those who do move into restaurant management than seek to determine why waitresses do not. There is also a danger in generalizing issues drawn from industrial or bureaucratic settings of diverting attention from matters of greater significance to other categories of workers. The limited research that has been done on service occupations to this point tends to concentrate on topics derived from research in industrial settings (for example, relations between supervisors and workers) and to rely on factory metaphors: insurance companies are "clerical work factories" (de Kadt 1984); flight attendants forced to serve more passengers in less time are subject to "speed-up" (Hochschild 1983:123); waitresses perceive customers as inanimate substance to be "processed" (discussed in Chapter 2). Though these metaphors are often instructive, reliance on a conceptual

13

framework drawn from industrial research leads in some cases to the neglect of features, such as interaction with the public, that distinguish service occupations from other types of work. William Whyte's (1977) study of human relations in the restaurant industry, for instance, focuses on interaction between co-workers, supervisors, and managers. Comparatively little is said about worker–customer interaction, though this is a critical relationship from the waitress's standpoint.

Even within the food service industry, it is difficult to generalize on the concerns and constraints of employees. At Route each waitress collects and keeps all her tips; but in some restaurants waitresses pool tips, while in others they are expected to *tip out* or transfer a percentage of their tips to the busboy, bartender, hostess, or dishwasher. There are waitresses who control all cash transactions with their customers and are personally liable for shortages, and waitresses whose tips are automatically included in the check as a percentage of the bill. Route waitresses perform virtually all tasks of serving themselves. Elsewhere, the business of serving is distributed across an entourage of support workers: hostesses, busboys, water servers, cocktail waitresses, and maitre d's. At Route there are no intermediate levels of supervision between waitresses and management, waitresses outrank hostesses, and among servers, seniority carries no formal benefits. Other restaurants designate headwaitresses and dining-room managers, have full-time hostesses who function as shift supervisors, and assign more lucrative stations to core or senior-ranking servers (see, for instance, Mars and Nicod 1984:68). In each case, variations in the way work is structured will be reflected in the nature of relations among waitresses, between waitresses, customers, and management, in the waitress's images of self, and in how she defines and defends her work interests. For this reason, any effort to understand the employee's orientation to work must examine her choices and preferred methods of action with reference to the distinctive structural constraints of her job. Structure and strategy must be approached as integrated systems.

Significance of Waitress as Research Subject

The spirit of resistance and determination exhibited by the Route waitress challenges images of women as passive and powerless that pervade much of the literature on women and work. In large part such images are byproducts of research that, in focusing on structural barriers to sexual parity, fails to explore the ways in which women recast or reject the exploitive processes to which they are subjected. The literature on sexist socialization practices tells us how women are "conditioned," "tracked," and "channeled" into traditional female fields. Analyses of discrimination describe the processes by which women are "restricted" and "excluded" from high-status positions, and "confined" and "crowded" into low-reward female occupations. But neither the theories nor the objectifying language in which they are expressed conveys a sense that women actively resist this circumscription of opportunities that so profoundly affects the quality of their lives (Paules 1990a). The waitress deserves our attention because she contests the notion of female passivity implicit in past research, demonstrating by her enterprising defiance that women may not, after all, "accept what is."

The waitress also warrants our interest because as a service worker, she is a member of the largest and fastest growing, yet least researched category of workers

15

in the United States. Following World War II, the United States became the first country in the world in which more than half the work force was employed in the service sector (Fuchs 1968:1). Over the last two decades, expansion of the service sector has proceeded at an unprecedented rate, with the overwhelming majority of new jobs created in service industries (W. Howe 1987; Rothman 1987). Today, the service sector employs more than three times the number of workers engaged in goods-production, and more than twenty-five times the number employed in agriculture (Koepp 1987). Growth of employment in service industries is expected to exceed growth in goods-production through the year 2000 (Kutscher 1987; Personick 1987).[10]

Despite, or perhaps because of the rapid expansion of the service sector, service industries have received little attention from social scientists, leading economists to designate them the "Cinderella industries of academics and politicians alike" and the "stepchild of economic research" (Gershuny and Miles 1983:10).[11] In sociology, research on services focuses on a limited group of professions or semiprofessions, with particular emphasis given to jobs in the health professions and education. When nonprofessional services are considered at all, it is typically obscure or morally ambiguous occupations that receive attention. Since its founding in 1974, *Work and Occupations* (formerly the *Sociology of Work and Occupations*) has published articles on male strippers, "taxi dancers," and butchers, but none on cashiers or hairdressers, one on salespersons (in a bread factory), and only two (both on waitresses) on food and beverage workers, though this group constitutes the largest category of service workers in the United States (U.S. Department of Labor, Bureau of Labor Statistics 1986). In contrast, twenty-eight articles on blue-collar (factory) workers have appeared in the journal. In general texts on the sociology and anthropology of work and occupations, discussions of blue-collar workers tend to precede discussions of direct services (defined later), if the latter are addressed at all.[12] Thus, despite the fact that "McDonald's has more employees than U.S. Steel" (George Will, quoted in Albrecht and Zemke 1985:1), social scientists continue to give blue-collar, and especially factory workers, precedence over direct-service workers.

It is probably because services are "extraordinarily underresearched" (Channon 1978:xv), that there is no consensus on the definition of service occupations. Often, service industries are defined in terms of what they are not, as reflected in the use of the terms *tertiary* and *residual* to refer to the service sector (Gershuny and Miles 1983:11). The Bureau of Labor Statistics defines the service-producing sector as everything not included in goods-production; that is, anything other than agriculture, manufacturing, mining, or construction (Rothman 1987:162). So defined, the service sector encompasses a wide range of occupations that have seemingly little in common. President of the United States, janitor, hairdresser, and zoologist have been grouped together as service occupations by commentators who see services as "jobs that do not seem to fit into any other category" (Koepp 1987).

Defining services in terms of what they are does not eliminate the incongruity of occupations grouped under service, which is, in fact, a heterogeneous category. Nonetheless, positive definitions provide a sense of what distinguishes services from other kinds of work. Victor Fuchs (1968:16) suggests that most service industries are populated by white-collar workers, are labor intensive, deal with consumers, and produce intangible products. Drawing on Robert Rothman (1987:162), this definition is further refined here to distinguish direct services, or service industries that deal with *customers* and *passengers,* from professions such as medicine and law that deal with *patients* and *clients,* and from occupations such as education, in which the service recipients are referred to neither as *customers* nor as *clients.* This distinction is particularly relevant when addressing issues of power and control, since power relations are generally thought to be reversed between service workers who have clients and those who have customers. The subordinate position of clients to those they depend on for knowledge and assistance is reflected in the term *client,* which recalls the feudal patron–client relationship (Gersuny and Rosengren 1973:136). Conversely, the subordinate position of direct-service providers to customers is implied in labels such as *server,* the contemporary term for waiters and waitresses.

A number of factors may explain the neglect of services by social scientists. The continued emphasis on blue-collar occupations may be the result of lag between the interests of the academic community and structural transformations in the labor force, though by now the gap should have started to close. It may be, too, that blue-collar workers continue to draw a disproportionate share of attention from social scientists, because the industrial working class has traditionally been viewed as a critical force for social change (Gershuny and Miles 1983:10). Direct-service jobs, in particular, may be passed over as potential subjects of investigation because they are typically held by teenagers, older workers, part-timers, and women (Albrecht and Zemke 1985; Fuchs 1968), who are perceived as marginal or peripheral workers. Researchers may hesitate to investigate services for fear they will contract the low status of these workers through some process of contagion. Alternatively, direct-service jobs such as hairdresser, shoe salesperson, and waitress may be perceived as trivial, and so unworthy of serious investigation, because the focus or product of these occupations—a new hairstyle, a new pair of shoes, a burger—is trivial. Finally, the association of direct services with such pleasurable pursuits as eating, drinking, traveling, and shopping may contribute to the low prestige, and hence neglect of service occupations, because work that looks least like play has traditionally been taken more seriously and valued more highly in American culture (Riesman 1953:300).

Whatever the source of neglect, direct-service jobs and service occupations in general are increasingly representative of the type of work performed by the majority of Americans and need to be understood. The lack of research on services is of particular significance for the study of women, as women have been consistently overrepresented in service industries (Fuchs 1985:320; Stanback et al. 1981:80). Investigation of waitressing, in many ways the prototypical service occupation, will begin to redress the long-standing neglect of service industries and so enhance our understanding of women's experience in postindustrial society.

Research Methods

Data for this study were obtained over an eighteen-month period employing the anthropological methodology of participant observation.[13] While participant observation is generally understood to refer to the researcher's long-term participation in and observation of the culture of the informant, the methodology also permits the informant to participate in the research process. In contrast to mainstream hypothesis-testing social sci-

ence, in which the informant's role is narrowly circumscribed by a framework developed by the researcher,
which the informant can neither modify nor transcend
(Agar 1980:68), the method of participant observation,
joined with the anthropological commitment to grasping
the native's point of view (Malinowski 1922:25), allows
those under study to contribute to the research—not
only in providing answers to prefabricated questions, but
in formulating the questions themselves. Those with
whom the anthropologist lives or works over an extended
period will necessarily help direct or redirect the course
of inquiry, if not consciously and explicitly, then by drawing attention to or away from specific issues by their
actions and language, by their repeated digressions from
or recurrence to particular subjects, or by their untam-
pered silence. The mutually participative character of the
anthropological approach was critical to the outcome of
this investigation, for as I took part in the work of the
waitress, she took part in transforming this work from an
examination of exploitation to an exploration of the many
ways in which the oppressed may reject their oppression.

On my part, participation in this study involved
waitressing at the restaurant two to five shifts a week, as
well as talking with informants over dinner, over shopping carts at the supermarket, and over the phone. Observation was carried out both in the course of shifts and
during occasional off-hour visits to the restaurant. Taped
interviews were conducted with twenty-one restaurant
employees drawn from all three shifts, including fourteen
waitresses, four managers, two waiters, and a cook.[14]
Interviews were loosely structured and in most cases
consisted in asking the informant to recount her or his
work history. Though research was confined to one restaurant, the majority of informants had worked at other
restaurants and spoke, during interviews and in the

course of work, on the basis of past as well as current employment experience.

Some waitresses are quoted more often than others in this text. The waitresses who are quoted most are those who have worked with the company longest, are familiar with the histories of quarrels and love affairs, which date back five and six years, can recount the comings and goings of long-departed managers, recall the price of a Number Two three summers ago, and describe long-discarded uniforms. They are also the workers who are most deeply enmeshed in restaurant politics and most intimate with the interpersonal mechanics of each shift. In focusing on these waitresses, whose adaptations to the constraints and pressures of their work are especially well developed, I may be charged with foregrounding a minority. Yet the women who speak most often in the following pages are those who are considered by customers, managers, and co-waitresses, and who consider themselves, the core workers in the restaurant. Their prominence in this study is a reflection of their centrality at Route.

2

"Getting" and "Making" a Tip

The waitress can't help feeling a sense of personal failure
and public censure when she is "stiffed."
—*William F. Whyte*, "When Workers and Customers Meet"

They're rude, they're ignorant, they're obnoxious,
they're inconsiderate. . . . Half these people don't deserve to come out and eat, let alone try and tip a waitress.
—*Route waitress*

The financial and emotional hazards inherent in
the tipping system have drawn attention from sociolo-
gists, and more recently anthropologists, concerned with
the study of work. In general these researchers have
concluded that workers who receive gratuities exercise
little control over the material outcome of tipping and
less over its symbolic implications. In his study of Chicago cabdrivers, Fred Davis (1959) found that drivers
employ diverse strategies to increase the odds of getting
a favorable tip, including padding fares with fictitious
charges (for example, charging for extra luggage); embar-
rassing a passenger into relinquishing a bigger tip by
creating a scene over making change; tailoring the ride to

23

fit the perceived temperament of the passenger (fast for businessmen, slow for old people); and subjecting passengers to hard-luck stories. In addition, cabdrivers develop typologies of passengers (the Sport, the Lady Shopper, Live Ones) in an effort to predict and explain the outcome of individual fares. Davis (1959:164) concludes, however, that "in the last analysis, neither the driver's typology of fares nor his stratagems further to any marked degree his control of the tip." A study of tipping among users of a suburban cab company in California (Karen 1962) revealed that the rendering of special services to passengers did not increase the likelihood of receiving a gratuity, and that on the whole tippers and nontippers are consistent in their tipping behavior. The driver's ability to control the outcome of a tip is thus presumably minimal.

Previous observations of restaurant servers support the thesis of limited worker control. Suellen Butler and William Snizek (1976) identify three strategies adopted by waitresses in an effort to manipulate the material rewards of their work: increased ritualization (exemplified by the wine ritual); friendly rapport or "buttering up" the customer; and product promotional activity, in which the waitress attempts to sell her customers more—and more expensive—menu items and so increase her 15 percent tip. While the authors were unable to investigate the efficacy of the first two strategies, they suggest that both are risky and largely ineffective. Only product promotional activity, which was directly tested by the authors, was found to be effective in increasing tip earnings.

Several observers of restaurant work have reported the existence of customer typologies similar to those used by cabdrivers. Gerald Mars and Michael Nicod (1984:54) note that waiters categorize customers on the basis of crosscutting criteria such as length of stay and size of party but comment that these systems of classification are "unpredictable" and "dependent on unreliable verbal and appearance clues." James Spradley and Brenda Mann provide an extensive list of customer types recognized by cocktail waitresses and note that "it was important to the waitresses to make such fine distinctions" (1975:61). There is some indication that servers adapt their performance to fit different categories of diners, but the control function, if any, of customer typologies remains unclear from the authors' descriptions.

While some attention has been directed toward the worker's ability to control the financial outcome of the tipping transaction, it has been assumed that the emotional hazards of tipping are an evil the server is helpless to combat. This view is most clearly expressed by Whyte who writes that "the waitress can't help feeling a sense of personal failure and public censure when she is 'stiffed'" (1946:129). His contention is substantiated by the testimony of his informants: a restaurant owner recalls a waitress who would occasionally break down and cry, "I failed . . . I failed today. After all I did for them, they didn't like me" (1946:129). A waiter comments:

> This tipping business is a great evil. You know, waiters have inferiority complexes. They are afraid to tell people they are a waiter. . . . It's the tipping system that does it. (Whyte 1977:372)

And a headwaiter observes:

> When they were calling each other mister, I said to them, "Look, you are no gentlemen. Gentlemen do not take tips. And therefore you should not call one another mister." It is this tipping

system that is the evil. That's the really degrading part of it. (Whyte 1977:372)

Along similar lines, Mars and Nicod (1984:74–75) report that overtipping may underscore the "socioeconomic superiority" of the customer, while disproportionately small tips may cause the server to feel "degraded, embarrassed, nonplussed, or otherwise upset." These comments suggest that servers adhere to a kind of symbolic illogic which compels them to interpret small and large tips alike as a negative reflection on themselves; thus, while a small tip is interpreted as an insult, a large tip is read not as a compliment, but as a sign of the server's social and economic subordination. Further, they suggest that servers perceive tips as symbolic statements about their personal qualities and social status.

Making a Tip at Route

A common feature of past research is that the worker's control over the tipping system is evaluated in terms of her efforts to con, coerce, compel, or otherwise manipulate a customer into relinquishing a bigger tip. Because these efforts have for the most part proven futile, the worker has been seen as having little defense against the financial vicissitudes of the tipping system. What these studies have overlooked is that an employee can increase her tip income by controlling the number as well as the size of tips she receives. This oversight has arisen from the tendency of researchers to concentrate narrowly on the relationship between server and served, while failing to take into account the broader organizational context in which this relationship takes place.

Like service workers observed in earlier studies,

waitresses at Route strive to boost the amount of individual gratuities by rendering special services and being especially friendly. As one waitress put it, "I'll sell you the world if you're in my station." In general though, waitresses at Route Restaurant seek to boost their tip income, not by increasing the amount of individual gratuities, but by increasing the number of customers they serve. They accomplish this (a) by securing the largest or busiest stations and working the most lucrative shifts; (b) by "turning" their tables quickly; and (c) by controlling the flow of customers within the restaurant.

Technically, stations at Route are assigned on a rotating basis so that all waitresses, including rookies, work fast and slow stations equally. Station assignments are listed on the work schedule that is posted in the office window where it can be examined by all workers on all shifts, precluding the possibility of blatant favoritism or discrimination. Yet a number of methods exist whereby experienced waitresses are able to circumvent the formal rotation system and secure the more lucrative stations for themselves. A waitress can trade assignments with a rookie who is uncertain of her ability to handle a fast station; she can volunteer to take over a large station when a *call-out* necessitates reorganization of station assignments;[1] or she can establish herself as the only waitress capable of handling a particularly large or chaotic station. Changes in station assignments tend not to be formally recorded, so inconsistencies in the rotation system often do not show up on the schedule. Waitresses on the same shift may notice of course that a co-worker has managed to avoid an especially slow station for many days, or has somehow ended up in the busiest station two weekends in a row, but the waitresses' code of noninterference (discussed in Chapter 6), inhibits them from openly objecting to such irregularities.

A waitress can also increase her tip income by working the more lucrative shifts. Because day is the busiest and therefore most profitable shift at Route, it attracts experienced, professional waitresses who are most concerned and best able to maximize their tip earnings. There are exceptions: some competent, senior-ranking waitresses are unable to work during the day due to time constraints of family or second jobs. Others choose not to work during the day despite the potential monetary rewards, because they are unwilling to endure the intensely competitive atmosphere for which day shift is infamous.

The acutely competitive environment that characterizes day shift arises from the aggregate striving of each waitress to maximize her tip income by serving the greatest possible number of customers. Two strategies are enlisted to this end. First, each waitress attempts to *turn* her tables as quickly as possible. Briefly stated, this means she takes the order, delivers the food, clears and resets a table, and begins serving the next party as rapidly as customer lingering and the speed of the kitchen allow. A seven-year veteran of Route describes the strategy and its rewards:

> What I do is I prebus my tables. When the people get up and go all I got is glasses and cups, pull off, wipe, set, and I do the table turnover. But see that's from day shift. See the girls on graveyard . . . don't understand the more times you turn that table the more money you make. You could have three tables and still make a hundred dollars. If you turn them tables.

As the waitress indicates, a large part of turning tables involves getting the table cleared and set for the next customer. During a rush, swing and grave waitresses tend to leave dirty tables standing, partly because they are less experienced and therefore less efficient, partly to avoid being given parties, or *sat*, when they are already behind. In contrast, day waitresses assign high priority to keeping their tables cleared and ready for customers. The difference in method reflects increased skill and growing awareness of and concern with money-making strategies.

A waitress can further increase her customer count by controlling the flow of customers within the restaurant. Ideally the hostess or manager running the front house rotates customers among stations, just as stations are rotated among waitresses.[2] Each waitress is given, or *sat*, one party at a time in turn so that all waitresses have comparable customer counts at the close of a shift. When no hostess is on duty, or both she and the manager are detained and customers are waiting to be seated, waitresses will typically seat incoming parties.

Whether or not a formal hostess is on duty, day waitresses are notorious for bypassing the rotation system by racing to the door and directing incoming customers to their own tables. A sense of the urgency with which this strategy is pursued is conveyed in the comment of one five-year veteran, "They'll run you down to get that person at the door, to seat them in their station." The competition for customers is so intense during the day that some waitresses claim they cannot afford to leave the floor (even to use the restroom) lest they return to find a co-worker's station filled at their expense. "In the daytime, honey," remarks an eight-year Route waitress, "in the daytime it's like pulling teeth. You got to stay on the floor to survive. To survive." It is in part because they do not want to lose customers and tips to their co-workers that waitresses do not take formal breaks. Instead, they rest and eat between waiting tables or during lulls in busi-

which all
benefits the ER

ness, returning to the floor intermittently to check on parties in progress and seat customers in their stations.

The fast pace and chaotic nature of restaurant work provide a cover for the waitress's aggressive pursuit of customers, since it is difficult for other servers to monitor closely the allocation of parties in the bustle and confusion of a rush. Still, it is not uncommon for waitresses to grumble to management and co-workers if they notice an obvious imbalance in customer distribution. Here again, the waitress refrains from directly criticizing her fellow servers, voicing her displeasure by commenting on the paucity of customers in her own station, rather than the overabundance of customers in the stations of certain co-waitresses. In response to these grumblings, other waitresses may moderate somewhat their efforts to appropriate new parties, and management may make a special effort to seat the disgruntled server favorably.

A waitress can also exert pressure on the manager or hostess to keep her station filled. She may, for instance, threaten to leave if she is not seated enough customers.

> I said, "Innes [a manager], I'm in [station] one and two. If one and two is not filled at all times from now until three, I'm getting my coat, my pocketbook, and I'm leaving." And one and two was filled, and I made ninety-five dollars.

Alternatively, she can make it more convenient for the manager or hostess to seat her rather than her co-workers, either by keeping her tables open (as described), or by taking extra tables. If customers are waiting to be seated, a waitress may offer to pick up parties in a station that is closed or, occasionally, to pick up parties in another waitress's station.[3] In attempting either strategy, but especially the latter, the waitress must be adept not only at

---

waiting tables, but in interpersonal restaurant politics. Autonomy and possession are of central concern to waitresses, and a waitress who offers to pick up tables outside her station must select her words carefully if she is to avoid being accused of invading her co-workers' territory. Accordingly, she may choose to present her bid for extra parties as an offer to help—the manager, another waitress, the restaurant, customers—rather than as a request.

The waitress who seeks to increase her tip income by maximizing the number of customers she serves may endeavor to cut her losses by refusing to serve parties that have stiffed her in the past. If she is a low-ranking waitress, her refusal is likely to be overturned by the manager. If she is an experienced and valuable waitress, the manager may ask someone else to take the party, assure the waitress he will take care of her (that is, pad the bill and give her the difference), or even pick up the party himself. Though the practice is far from common, a waitress may go so far as to demand a tip from a customer who has been known to stiff in the past.

This party of two guys come in and they order thirty to forty dollars worth of food . . . and they stiff us. Every time. So Kaddie told them, "If you don't tip us, we're not going to wait on you." They said, "We'll tip you." So Kaddie waited on them, and they tipped her. The next night they came in, I waited on them and they didn't tip me. The third time they came in [the manager] put them in my station and I told [the manager] straight up, "I'm not waiting on them. . . ." So he made Hailey pick them up. And they stiffed Hailey. So when they came in the next night . . . [they] said, "Are you going to give us a table?" I said, "You going to tip me? I'm not going to wait on

---

you. You got all that money, you sell all that crack on the streets and you come here and you can't even leave me a couple bucks?" . . . So they left me a dollar. So when they come in Tuesday night, I'm telling them a dollar ain't enough.

The tactics employed by waitresses, and particularly day-shift waitresses, to increase their customer count and thereby boost their tip earnings have earned them a resounding notoriety among their less competitive co-workers. Day (and some swing) waitresses are described as "money hungry," "sneaky little bitches," "self-centered," "aggressive," "backstabbing bitches," and "cutthroats over tables." The following remarks of two Route waitresses, however, indicate that those who employ these tactics see them as defensive, not aggressive measures. A sense of the waitress's preoccupation with autonomy and with protecting what is hers also emerges from these comments.

You have to be like that. Because if you don't be like that, people step on you. You know, like as far as getting customers. I mean, you know, I'm sorry everybody says I'm greedy. I guess that's why I've survived this long at Route. Cause I am greedy. . . . *I want what's mine*, and if it comes down to me cleaning your table or my table, I'm going to clean my table. Because see I went through all that stage where I would do your table. To be fair. And you would walk home with seventy dollars, and I'd have twenty-five, cause I was being fair all night. (emphasis added)

If the customer comes in the door and I'm there getting that door, don't expect me to cover your

backside while you in the back smoking a cigarette and I'm here working for myself. You not out
there working for me. . . . When I go to the door
and get the customers, when I keep my tables
clean and your tables are dirty, and you wonder
why you only got one person . . . then that's just
tough shit. . . . You're damn right my station is
filled. *I'm not here for you.* (emphasis added)

Whether the waitress who keeps her station filled
with customers is acting aggressively or defensively, her
tactics are effective. It is commonly accepted that determined day waitresses make better money than less competitive co-workers even when working swing or grave.
Moreover Nera, the waitress most infamous for her relentless use of "money-hungry" tactics, is at the same
time most famous for her consistently high daily takes.
While other waitresses jingle change in their aprons,
Nera is forced to store wads of bills in her shoes and in
paper bags to prevent tips from overflowing her pockets.
She claims to make a minimum of five hundred dollars a
week in tip earnings; her record for one day's work ex-
ceeds two hundred dollars and is undoubtedly the record
for the restaurant.

Inverting the Symbolism of Tipping

It may already be apparent that the waitress
views the customer—not as a master to pamper and
appease—but as substance to be processed as quickly
and in as large a quantity as possible. The difference in
perspective is expressed in the objectifying terminology
of waitresses: a customer or party is referred to as a *table*,
or by table number, as *table five* or simply *five;* serv-

ing successive parties at a table is referred to as *turning the table;* taking an order is also known as *picking up a table;* and to serve water, coffee, or other beverages is to *water, coffee,* or *beverage* a table, number, or customer. Even personal acquaintances assume the status of inanimate matter, or tip-bearing plants, in the language of the server:

> I got my fifth-grade teacher [as a customer] one time. . . . I kept her coffeed. I kept her boyfriend coked all night. Sodaed. . . . And I kept them filled up.

If the customer is perceived as material that is processed, the goal of this processing is the production or extraction of a finished product: the tip. This image too is conveyed in the language of the floor. A waitress may comment that she "got a good tip" or "gets good tips," but she is more likely to say that she "made" or "makes good tips." She may also say that she "got five bucks out of" a customer, or complain that some customers "don't want to give up on" their money. She may accuse a waitress who stays over into her shift of "tapping on" her money, or warn an aspiring waitress against family restaurants on the grounds that "there's no money in there." In all these comments (and all are actual), the waitress might as easily be talking about mining for coal or drilling for oil as serving customers.

Predictably, the waitress's view of the customer as substance to be processed influences her perception of the meaning of tips, and especially substandard tips. At Route, low tips and stiffs are not interpreted as a negative reflection on the waitress's personal qualities or social status. Rather, they are felt to reveal the refractory nature or poor quality of the raw material from which the tip is extracted, produced, or fashioned. In less metaphorical terms, a low tip or stiff is thought to reflect the negative qualities and low status of the customer who is too cheap, too poor, too ignorant, or too coarse to leave an appropriate gratuity.[4] In this context, it is interesting to note that *stiff*, the term used in restaurants to refer to incidents of nontipping or to someone who does not tip, has also been used to refer to a wastrel or penniless man (Partridge 1984), a hobo, tramp, vagabond, deadbeat, and a moocher (Wentworth and Flexner 1975).[5]

Evidence that waitresses assign blame for poor tips to the tipper is found in their reaction to being undertipped or stiffed. Rather than breaking down in tears and lamenting her "personal failure," the Route waitress responds to a stiff by announcing the event to her co-workers and managers in a tone of angry disbelief. Co-workers and managers echo the waitress's indignation and typically ask her to identify the party (by table number and physical description), or if she has already done so, to be more specific. This identification is crucial for it allows sympathizers to join the waitress in analyzing the cause of the stiff, which is assumed a priori to arise from some shortcoming of the party, not the waitress. The waitress and her co-workers may conclude that the customers in question were rude, troublemakers, or bums, or they may explain their behavior by identifying them as members of a particular category of customers. It might be revealed for instance, that the offending party was a church group: church groups are invariably tightfisted. It might be resolved that the offenders were senior citizens, Southerners, or businesspeople: all well-known cheapskates. If the customers were European, the stiff will be attributed to ignorance of the American tipping system; if they were young, to immaturity; if they had children, to lack of funds.

These classifications and their attendant explanations are neither fixed nor trustworthy. New categories are invented to explain otherwise puzzling incidents, and all categories are subject to exception. Though undependable as predictive devices, customer typologies serve a crucial function: they divert blame for stiffs and low tips from the waitress to the characteristics of the customer. It is for this reason that it is "important" for workers to distinguish between different categories of customers, despite the fact that such distinctions are based on "unreliable verbal and appearance clues." In fact, it is precisely the unreliability, or more appropriately the flexibility, of customer typologies that makes them valuable to waitresses. When categories can be constructed and dissolved on demand, there is no danger that an incident will fall outside the existing system of classification and hence be inexplicable.

While waitresses view the customer as something to be processed and the tip as the product of this processing, they are aware that the public does not share their understanding of the waitress–diner–tip relationship. Waitresses at Route recognize that many customers perceive them as needy creatures willing to commit great feats of service and absorb high doses of abuse in their anxiety to secure a favorable gratuity or protect their jobs. They are also aware that some customers leave small tips with the intent to insult the server and that others undertip on the assumption that for a Route waitress even fifty cents will be appreciated. One waitress indicated that prior to being employed in a restaurant, she herself subscribed to the stereotype of the down-and-out waitress "because you see stuff on television, you see these wives or single ladies who waitress and they live in slummy apartments or slummy houses and they dress in rags." It is these images of neediness and desperation, which run so strongly against the waitress's perception of herself and her position, that she attacks when strained relations erupt into open conflict.

> Five rowdy black guys walked in the door and they went to seat themselves at table seven. I said, "Excuse me. You all got to wait to be seated." "We ain't got to do *shit*. We here to eat. . . ." So they went and sat down. And I turned around and just looked at them. And they said, "Well, I hope you ain't our waitress, cause you blew your tip. Cause you ain't getting nothing from us." And I turned around and I said, "You need it more than I do, baby."[6]

This waitress's desire to confront the customer's assumption of her destitution is widely shared among service workers whose status as tipped employees marks them as needy in the eyes of their customers. Davis (1959:162–63) reports that among cabdrivers "a forever repeated story is of the annoyed driver, who, after a grueling trip with a Lady Shopper, hands the coin back, telling her, 'Lady, keep your lousy dime. You need it more than I do.'" Mars and Nicod (1984:75) report a hotel waitress's claim that "if she had served a large family with children for one or two weeks, and then was given a 10p piece, she would give the money back, saying, 'It's all right, thank you, I've got enough change for my bus fare home.'" In an incident I observed (not at Route), a waitress followed two male customers out of a restaurant calling, "Excuse me! You forgot this!" and holding up the coins they had left as a tip. The customers appeared embarrassed, motioned for her to keep the money, and continued down the sidewalk. The waitress, now standing in the outdoor seating area of the restaurant and observed by curious diners, threw the money after the retreating men and returned to her work. Episodes such as these allow the worker to repudiate openly the evaluation of her financial status that is implied in an offensively small gratuity, and permit her to articulate her own understanding of what a small tip says and about whom. If customers can only afford to leave a dime, or feel a 10p piece is adequate compensation for two weeks' service, they must be very hard up or very ignorant indeed.

In the following incident the waitress interjects a denial of her neediness into an altercation that is not related to tipping, demonstrating that the customer's perception of her financial status is a prominent and persistent concern for her.

> She [a customer] wanted a California Burger with mayonnaise. And when I got the mayonnaise, the mayonnaise had a little brown on it. . . . So this girl said to me, she said, "What the fuck is this you giving me?" And I turned around, I thought, "Maybe she's talking to somebody else in the booth with her." And I turned around and I said, "Excuse me?" She said, "You hear what I said. I said, 'What the fuck are you giving me?'" And I turned around, I said, "I don't know if you're referring your information to *me,*" I said, "but if you're referring your information to *me,*" I said, "I don't *need* your bullshit." I said, "I'm not going to even take it. . . . Furthermore, I could care less if you eat or *don't* eat. . . . And you see this?" And I took her check and I ripped it apart. . . . And I took the California Burger and I says, "You don't have a problem anymore now, right?" She went up to the manager. And she says, "That black waitress"—I says, "Oh. By the way, what is

my name? I don't have a name, [using the words] 'that black waitress'. . . . My name happens to be Nera. . . . That's N-E-R-A. . . . And I don't need your bullshit, sweetheart. . . . People like you I can walk on, because you don't know how to talk to human beings." And I said, "I don't need you. I don't need your quarters. I don't need your nickels. I don't need your dimes. So if you want service, be my guest. Don't you *ever* sit in my station, cause I won't wait on you." The manager said, "Nera, please. Would you wait in the back?" I said, "No. I don't take back seats no more for nobody."

In each of these cases, the waitress challenges the customer's definition of the relationship in which tipping occurs. By speaking out, by confronting the customer, she demonstrates that she is not subservient or in fear of losing her job; that she is not compelled by financial need or a sense of social hierarchy to accept abuse from customers; that she does not, in Nera's words, "take back seats no more for nobody." At the same time, she reverses the symbolic force of the low tip, converting a statement on her social status or work skills into a statement on the tipper's cheapness or lack of savoir faire.

Symbolic Dimensions of Tipping

Of 1.5 million restaurant servers employed in the United States, 90 percent are women who receive at least two-thirds of their earnings in the form of gratuities (Butler and Skipper 1980:489). For some waitresses the fact that tips have traditionally gone un- or underreported and therefore un- or undertaxed contributes to their economic appeal, despite the adverse consequences of underreporting for social security and unemployment benefits (L. Howe 1977:123).[7] For others, the immediacy of tipping income is its central redeeming factor. "Waiting and waitressing is a MAC card," a Route waiter commented. "You walk in, you punch in your five hours of work, you walk out, you got forty bucks in your hand." For those whose financial needs are often small but urgent, the fast cash factor of the tipping system may be more valuable than the security of a steady weekly wage. This was the case for a seventeen-year-old hostess at Route who justified her demand to be trained for the floor partly on the grounds that if she were a waitress, whenever her baby needed something (Pampers, for example), she could come in and make the money by the end of her shift.

But a tip is more than payment for service rendered; it is a potent symbol capable of evoking a profound sense of triumph or provoking an angry blitz of expletives. It is, moreover, a symbol that embodies in coarse, even vulgar material form the myriad whisperings of power and control that pervade the server–served relationship. For this reason, careful examination of the symbolic potential of the tip is of relevance to the study of all service relationships—including those in which tipping does not occur.

Tip as Evaluative Device

The most salient symbolic function of the tip is that of evaluating the quality of service received by the consumer. Such a function is implied in the following passage from an article subtitled "Ten Commandments for All Food Servers":

> If the service is just OK, I usually leave a 10 percent tip. If the service is good, I leave 15

percent. But if the server has gone out of his or
her way, or I think the service was excellent, I
leave 20 percent. (Jerome n.d.)[8]

It is important to note that quality of service is increasingly bound up with the personal qualities of the employee: her ability to smile sincerely, to project an appropriate image (sexy, sophisticated, fun-loving), to harness
or suppress private emotions and so cultivate a desired
mood in the customer (Hochschild 1983). In assessing the
caliber of service, therefore, customers also appraise the
personality of the server. They are flattered by her smile
and applaud her with 30 percent. They are offended by
her terseness and censure her with thirty cents.

Though Robert Karen's (1962) study of cab passengers suggests that many customers do not calibrate
the size of a gratuity to reflect the quality of service, most
are aware, even without the guidance of journalists, that
it is their prerogative to do so. The evaluative capacity of
the tip may thus be said to constitute what Victor Turner
(1975:176) refers to as a manifest sense of the symbol. In
addition, the tip possesses what Turner refers to as latent
meanings "of which the subject is only marginally aware."
It is unlikely that either customer or waitress is conscious
of the resemblance for instance, but the tip bears strong
likeness to a gift both in the way it is handled and in its
potential implications for the status of server and served.

Tip as Gift

The origin of the word *tip* as used in service
contexts remains uncertain. Some contend that it is an
acronym for the edict "To Insure Prompt Service" that
was reportedly displayed on a box for customer donations
in a London coffeehouse. Those complying with the edict
by placing a contribution in the box received immediate

service (Butler and Skipper 1980:490; cf. Morris and
Morris 1977). While gratifyingly coherent, the legitimacy
of this derivation is doubtful. A more likely explanation is
that *tip* derives from *stipend* and ultimately from the
Latin *stips,* meaning *gift* (Morris and Morris 1977:567).
This derivation of *tip* accords well with its current definition as given in the *Oxford English Dictionary:*

> **Tip,** . . . A small present of money given to an
> inferior, esp. to a servant or employee of another
> for a service rendered or expected; a gratuity, a
> douceur.

Past researchers of restaurant work have also found it
appropriate to equate the tip with a gift, and the tipping
transaction with gift exchange.

> Like the universal gift, the tip received for service
> may normally be expected, but can never be de-
> manded. . . . Something given—service—must
> typically be returned with something of equiva-
> lent value—a tip. . . . It cannot be pressed for as
> an economic right. (Mars and Nicod 1984:75)

The comparison with gift exchange is under-
rather than overdrawn. It might further be noted that the
transfer of the tip, like the exchange of *vagua* in the Kula,
as described by Bronislaw Malinowski (1922:81), is "regulated by a set of traditional rules and conventions," and
that these conventions are themselves similar. In the
Kula, a system of Melanesian tribal exchange, "though
the valuable has to be handed over by the giver, the
receiver hardly takes any notice of it, and seldom receives
it actually into his hands" (1922:352). This convention,
Malinowski suggests, reflects the recipient's "reluctance

to appear in want of anything" and more generally, the "very human and understandable attitude of disdain at the reception of a gift" (1922:353).

Like the valuable, the tip is rarely received directly from the hand of the giver. It is left on the table, nudged under the sugar caddy or slipped between the salt and pepper, to be retrieved by the waitress when the customer is out of sight. Reluctant to appear in want, the waitress, like the Kula participant, accepts the gift with "nonchalance and disdain," sweeping it into her pocket while removing dirty plates and crumpled napkins, as though her chief concern were to clear the table of excess clutter.

Despite these parallels, the ritual of tipping differs from gift exchange in an important respect. As noted, the exchange of gifts demands that something given be returned with something of equal value. But what the waitress gives, namely service, cannot be described as a gift, for a gift is by definition voluntary (ostensibly at least), while the delivery of service is a formal duty of the waitress's job. For this reason, the transfer of a tip is more accurately compared to unilateral gift-giving than to gift exchange. In this connection it is significant that *gratuity,* a synonym for *tip,* shares Latin roots with *gratuitous* defined as follows:

> 1. Freely bestowed or obtained; granted without claim or merit; provided without payment or return; costing nothing to the recipient; free. (*Oxford English Dictionary*)

For fulfilling duties that she has explicitly contracted to perform and for which she is already paid by another party, the waitress receives from the customer a tip, a gratuity, a gift.

The implications of unilateral gift-giving for the respective statuses of donor and recipient are illustrated in an analysis of gift-giving in a different service context. In her study of present-day household workers, Judith Rollins (1985) found that women frequently make presents of used clothes and furniture to their domestic servants. The custom, which dates at least to the seventeenth century, originally had economic motivation, as gifts were given in place of wages (Rollins 1985:191; see also Sutherland 1981:112–13). In its current use, the symbolic implications of unilateral gift-giving overshadow its material significance. Quoting Marcel Mauss (1925), Rollins explains:

> To give is to show one's superiority, to show that one is something more and higher. . . . To accept without returning or repaying more is to face subordination, to become a client and subservient. (1985:192)

In conferring gifts that are not reciprocated, the employer shows that she is "something more and higher" than the domestic who accepts without repaying more. In the same way, customers confirm and emphasize their superiority to the waitress who receives their gratuities—gratis.

The symbolic force of the unilateral gift may be still more potent than suggested by Rollins. In service work and conceivably also in domestic service, the transfer of a gift can invert as well as reinforce status relations operating outside the service context. Such a situation is described by Frances Donovan in her firsthand account of waitressing in Chicago.

> Presently two mail carriers came in, one white and one colored, and each, when he left, gave me

a dime. I had tipped colored boys many times but it was indeed a new experience to have one tip me. (1920:194)

That Donovan regards the African-American tipper as her inferior is indicated both by her acknowledgment of the incident as noteworthy, and by her reference to the carrier, who is presumably an adult, as a "boy." Through the act of tipping, the "boy" inverts status relations operating outside the restaurant and asserts his superiority—however restricted in time and space—to Donovan. The same opportunity for status inversion exists between all tipped employees and customers whom they consider their social or economic inferiors. The ambivalence experienced by the server in this situation is conveyed in Donovan's description of the first tip she received as a waitress.

A shabby, dissipated wreck of a man came in and sat down on one of the stools at my counter. To my surprise, he ordered a forty-five-cent meal. I became very busy and I did not at once remove his dirty dishes. A boy sat down on the stool vacated by this man and I took his order. When I was attempting to clear a place for it, I saw a greasy, dirty nickel on the counter. The boy gave it a little push towards me and said, "I guess this is yours." (1920:194)

Donovan does not explicitly recount her reaction to the episode; nor does she need to. It is evident from her description that she is uncomfortable with receiving a "greasy, dirty nickel" from a "shabby, dissipated wreck," and it can be inferred that her discomfort arises from the recognition that the normative social order has been violated, and her position therein threatened.

"Getting" and *"Making"* a Tip

As Rollins (1985) points out, the quality of the gift conferred upon the worker, whether a greasy nickel or hand-me-down clothes, reinforces the declaration of status difference conveyed in the act of giving itself. In the case of the domestic,

> the employer, in giving old clothes and furniture and leftover food, is transmitting to the servant the employer's perception of the servant as needy, unable to provide adequately for herself, and willing to accept others' devalued goods. (1985:193)

In the restaurant, the quantity rather than the quality of the gift is the decisive variable, but the effect is the same. Like the discarded shoes, dead flowers, and soggy salad bestowed upon domestics, the pennies and dimes left among the dirty plates for the waitress carry an implicit devaluation of her status and life quality. Penny pails are now placed in front of cash registers to spare customers the annoyance of pocketing the troublesome coin; yet pennies are considered appropriate gifts for women who wait tables. The symbolic statement is clear: so down, so destitute is the waitress that she will be pleased to accept what to the customer is bothersome change.

In drawing attention to the waitress's ability to subvert this complex and potentially degrading symbolism and moderate the financial risks of tipping, my purpose has been to demonstrate the waitress's power of resistance, her spirit of defiance, and her ability to manipulate her work environment to protect her interests. It has not been my intention to question the exploitive nature of a system of compensation that compels women to compete against one another to secure a fair wage, and absolves employers from responsibility for the economic security of workers from whose labor they profit. Nor has it been the aim of this discussion to suggest that waitresses are immune to the financial and emotional dangers of the tipping system. However skillfully the waitress maximizes her customer count, she remains vulnerable to the vicissitudes of the food service industry. Route servers suffered periodic drops in their tip income because of seasonal fluctuations in customer volume and unexpected slumps in business, as when the restaurant stood nearly empty for three weeks while road construction obscured the entrance to the parking lot. Likewise, though waitresses blame their customers and not themselves for low tips, being stiffed or undertipped remains an emotionally taxing experience. At Route as elsewhere, the failure of a customer to provide adequate compensation for service was the frequent cause of impassioned outbursts. Nonetheless, throughout the course of research and in five years' prior experience waiting tables, I never encountered a waitress who interpreted a bad tip as a "personal failure." What tears were shed were shed in anger, not in self-rebuke.

3

The Limits of Managerial Authority

You are the cog and the beltline of the bureaucratic machinery itself; you are a link in the chains of commands, persuasions, notices, bills, which bind together the men who make decisions and the men who make things; . . . Your authority is confined strictly within a prescribed orbit of occupational actions, and such power as you wield is a borrowed thing. Yours is the subordinate's mark. . . . You are the servant of decision, the assistant of authority.
—*C. Wright Mills*, White Collar

Researchers of automobile workers, waitresses, and other low-status workers have typically assumed that movement into foremanship or management is a goal both desired and desirable. Accordingly, when these workers at the bottom—workers who have no place to go but up—resist, reject, or disparage advancement, it is assumed that some deficiency of ambition or confidence or some lack of opportunity is at fault. The alternative possibility, that jobs higher up are no longer worth moving "up" into is rarely taken into serious consideration. Such a possibility is suggested, however, by the literature on the disempowerment of first-line supervisory positions, and in particular, by investigations into the effects of centralization and unionization on the authority of the industrial foreman.[1]

Foreman: Middle Man, Marginal Man

Researchers in industrial settings have described foremen as "men in the middle" (Whyte and Gardner 1945) and "marginal men" (Wray 1949). The first description refers to the foreman's position between higher management and rank-and-file workers, in which he is subject to demands and criticism from above and below, or forced to "take it from both sides" (Whyte and Gardner 1945:19). The second refers to the marginalization of the foreman from the decision-making process, a consequence of the centralization of the decision-making function at higher levels in the organization, the development of highly specialized staff departments, and the growth of unionized labor (Chinoy 1955; Mills 1956). The conjoined influence of centralization and unionization has created a situation in modern industry in which

> issues are settled between union representatives and higher management, and the foreman is expected simply to conform to the joint decisions of these representatives. . . . The foreman must be viewed as the recipient of union–management agreement or conflict rather than as a positive contributor to union–management relations. (Wray 1949:300)

In some organizations, the foreman may not attend union–management meetings (Wray 1949) and may receive information concerning new policies—policies he is charged to implement—from the shop steward or other workers under his supervision (Whyte and Gardner 1945:24).

The foreman's authority has been further undercut by the development of specialized staff departments, which have taken over many functions traditionally associated with the role of foreman, including control over the hiring and firing of employees and over the setting of rates for different jobs (Whyte and Gardner 1945:20–22). In addition to narrowing the foreman's scope of authority, the transfer of these functions to specialists deprives the foreman of the prestige that attends power. The fact that foremen may be paid less than nonsupervisory workers also diminishes the prestige of their position. The foreman's meager pay is a consequence of his classification as an executive, in which capacity he works for salary and is not compensated for the overtime which inevitably accompanies the assumption of increased responsibility (Whyte and Gardner 1945:24).

Despite his marginalization from the decision-making process, the circumscription of his authority by specialized staff departments and unions, and his loss of prestige, the foreman continues to be identified by management as part of the managerial line (Mills 1956:91). Beyond the factory gates too, the foreman has traditionally been regarded as one elevated above the rank and file; one who enjoys the personal and monetary rewards of executive status (Chinoy 1955:44). The disjuncture between these images and the reality of the foreman's role inspires feelings of insecurity and resentment among foremen who are apt to consider themselves "special victims of the disparity between social norms and social reality" (Wray 1949:301). Efforts by foremen to unionize indicate the extent to which they feel threatened by the mounting constraints and contradictions of their position. To the degree that unionization represents an attempt to "rejoin the men," this strategy of self-protection also suggests that foremen do not fully accept company assurances that "executive and supervisory management are one" (Mills 1956:91).

The Restaurant Manager:
Middle Man, Marginal Man, Fill-in Man

The restaurant manager has suffered a fate in many ways similar to that of the industrial foreman. Like the foreman, the manager is caught in the middle of and yet excluded from relations between higher-level management and rank-and-file workers. He too has been marginalized from the decision-making process and has suffered a loss of prestige as a result of the diminished power and rewards associated with his position. Because the service sector remains largely unorganized (U.S. Department of Labor 1975), the restaurant manager's authority is less likely to be restricted by the presence of unions. However, the tipping system and the responsibilities of fill-in man impose comparable constraints on the manager's power of action.

Centralization

Each of the more than twelve hundred Route restaurants scattered across the thoroughfares of the United States is tied to a central office in California. There are intermediate links between California and individual restaurants: unit managers answer to district managers, district managers to regional managers—but these links function primarily as conduits for policies formulated by executives at headquarters. It is California that determines the amount of salt to be added to chicken gravy and the color of the apron dishwashers will wear, as well as more vital issues: how much a starting cook will earn an hour, what type of benefits package the company will offer. The ostensible objective of centralization is consistency and efficiency. Customers dining at Route in Florida can expect to receive the same optimally prepared sirloin tips, warmed at the same optimally determined temperature that they ordered while traveling in Arizona. A cook moving from Florida to Arizona can expect to serve the same tips at the same temperature at his new, but comfortingly familiar job.

A consequence, and some neo-Marxists would contend the central objective of centralization, is the disempowerment of employees and all but the highest-ranking managers. By transferring control over the decisions of work from employee to "expert," the company divests workers of knowledge and skills that once made them disturbingly indispensable, and thwarts their natural inclination to work below potential (Braverman 1974). The separation of conception and execution, which heralds the deskilling of labor, is particularly vivid at Route, where the division is realized materially in the vast geographic distances that frequently divide those who think from those who do. The success of centralization and the attendant process of routinization is revealed in the amazing (or alarming) similarity of Route restaurants so widely separated from the central office and from each other.

The effects of centralization and routinization are most commonly associated with rank-and-file workers, and the assembly-line worker in the automobile factory is typically held up as the classic victim of deskilling. Yet the foreman is also a victim of centralization; indeed, the deskilling of labor necessarily implies the deskilling of the supervisor who is condemned to monitor those who monitor the machines. Similarly in the restaurant, centralization accompanied by a campaign of routinization aimed largely at wage workers has reduced first-line managers to mere "servants of decisions" in the most trivial matters. The number of crackers to be stocked in a cracker basket, the ounces of gravy to be ladled onto noodles, the day on which chicken soup and corn will be served instead of pea soup and mixed vegetables—these decisions are handed down to the manager in order that he may in turn hand them down to his employees. He is told what to tell his workers to wear, what to allow them to eat, when and how to reward them for loyalty to the company. The steak knives, the brand of mayonnaise, the number of steps between the grill and fryer should be similar in each of the company's twelve hundred units; and so too should be the greetings, uniforms, and smiles of the workers who use the knives and mayonnaise. The manager's role is not to innovate, but to maintain this carefully manufactured uniformity; not to lead and inspire his workers, but to reproduce a prototype.

The Tipping System

John Henderson (1965:61) proposes that workers who receive the greater portion of their income in the form of gratuities are more accurately described as private entrepreneurs than employees in the traditional sense. Observations at Route indicate that those who supervise tipped employees cannot be considered managers in the traditional sense. In transferring control over the waitress's income to the public, the tipping system divests management of a traditional source and symbol of managerial authority and detracts from the employee's sense of obligation toward the company and those who represent it. In this respect too, the restaurant manager is in a position similar to that of the industrial foreman whose control over his workers' income has been mitigated by the growth of unions and specialized personnel departments. The manager's position may be the more precarious of the two, in that the tipping system provides employees with the incentive as well as the freedom to pursue their interests at the expense of the company he is charged to represent.

Proponents of the tipping system contend that employees would be less industrious, courteous, or meticulous if they worked for a flat wage or, alternatively, if a service charge were automatically added to the bill as under the European system (Citron 1989). According to this argument, the tipping system provides built-in incentive for employees to work their hardest, for the harder they work, the more they earn. By the same token it might be argued that tipping relieves management of the burden of motivating employees to work, and that under the tipping system managers will have less cause to reproach or penalize employees for lack of diligence.

The effects of the tipping system on the manager's position are very different from those implied in the natural-incentive argument. The waitress's financial independence from her employer releases her from many conventional constraints of the employee role. She feels little motivation to feign veneration or conceal contempt for an employer whose claim to her allegiance is not sustained by financial incentive. Nor does she feel compelled to comply closely with company policy, particularly when it interferes with her tip-earning ability. It is true that the prospect of eliciting more and bigger gratuities motivates the waitress to work hard, but she works in her own interests, not in the interests of management. In some cases waitress and manager concerns coincide, and it matters little whether the waitress's industry is motivated by self-interest or a sense of obligation invoked by financial dependence. Both the waitress and management, for instance, generally profit from moving as many customers through the restaurant as quickly as possible and are able to work harmoniously toward this goal.

Just as often, waitress and manager interests conflict or are simply not connected. For example, waitresses do not like to take to-go orders, because they take time away from their table parties, and people who order takeout rarely leave tips. Takeout orders are also aggravating because they need to be packaged in special disposable containers with disposable silverware and carryout condiments—all of which are frequently out of stock, not in the right place, or not carried by the restaurant. Because of this, waitresses are forced to pack banana splits and dinner salads in segmented dinner cartons, and serve butter, syrup, and salad dressing in large coffee cups. To avoid losing time and patience on this unprofitable pursuit, waitresses keep takeout customers waiting at the register or on the phone until their other (tipping) customers have been taken care of and discourage customers from making a habit of ordering food to go by freely expressing their exasperation when processing to-go orders. For the restaurant, this means a loss of future business from customers who go away with a bad impression of Route's service and vow never to return—for takeout or table service.

A second example of conflict is found in the waitress's desire to maximize tip income as opposed to the manager's overriding concern with cost control. In an effort to elicit larger tips, a waitress may provide her customers with oversized portions of sour cream, extra rolls, free desserts or drinks—whatever she can procure without writing a check. In return for her generosity, offered at the manager's expense, she will ideally receive larger gratuities, either because her customers have more money left over since they were not charged for extras, or because her plenteous portions left a general impression of good service, or possibly because customers understand that she has cheated the company on their behalf. In fulfilling the desire of customers to get more and pay less, of course, the waitress compromises the manager's desire to minimize food costs and maximize revenues.

In addition, waitresses occasionally refuse to "sell" menu items that are troublesome to serve. Making milk shakes is a time-consuming and exasperating process: the ice cream is always too hard or too soft, and the shake can unfailingly flies off the mixer at high speed spraying all within a two-foot radius with milk and syrup. To avoid making shakes, waitresses at one Route unit responded to all requests for the irksome item with the declaration that the shake machine was broken.[2] A waitress may also decline to offer items that are repeatedly sent back to the kitchen, are difficult to stack, take a long time to prepare, or annoy the cooks. In this way she saves herself time, reduces the chances that her customers will be dissatisfied with the food or the wait, and maintains good standing with the kitchen—all strategies that ultimately help increase her tip earnings. In so pursuing her own interests, the waitress undermines the company's goal of diversifying the menu and impedes the manager's ability to realize this goal.

The waitress's inclination to pursue her interests at the expense of the company gains impetus from her conviction that since management does not provide her income, she is not obliged to comply with its dictates. Both the amount and the form of payment the waitress receives at the hand of management contribute to her perception that she is not paid by the company. At Route, income tax as well as medical and life insurance payments are calculated on the basis of wages and declared tips combined, but are deducted only from the waitress's paycheck, since tips go directly into her pocket and are therefore beyond the company's (and government's) reach. As a result, a waitress who pulls in $60 to $120 a day in tips may receive a paycheck for less than $10, or even for zero dollars, showing the appropriate deductions. The receipt of these checks more often evokes mockery than gratitude from the waitress; she is inclined to feign concern over stowing her $6 check in a safe place or express exasperation at the manager's insistence on delivering a check for seventy-five cents. Understandably, Route waitresses do not include their wages when asked to calculate how much they make, and a waitress occasionally turns up a two-year-old check she has simply forgotten to cash. A paycheck, one waitress commented, is just "an extra tip." For most waitresses, it is a tip too small to count.

An atmosphere of jocularity can also be created by the conferral of a raise. After announcing her good fortune to her co-workers, the rewarded waitress may calculate how much the extra nickel or dime an hour will increase her daily, weekly, or annual income, then enumerate the clothes she will buy and bills she will pay with her newfound wealth. Like the rejection of small tips, this ritual disparagement allows the waitress to proclaim her financial well-being and challenge popular images of the waitress as destitute. Beyond this, by belittling her raise and $10 check, the waitress underscores, in loud and scornful tones, the company's lack of power over her and her co-workers.

The form of payment the waitress receives from management further diminishes her sense of financial dependence upon and obligation to the company. The waitress who works for tips is accustomed to receiving tangible and preferably immediate payment for her labor: this applies not only to work accomplished for her customers, but for work performed for fellow employees.[3] If a waitress wants to leave the restaurant before her last party has finished eating, she offers to pay a fellow waitress to clear the table for her, either by telling her to keep the tip, or by offering her a dollar outright. She may also offer to pay a fellow waitress to take over some part of her sidework she cannot or does not want to complete. In this ready-cash–oriented environment the manager's position is predictably weak. Not only is the paycheck he offers as payment inadequate, it is delayed and is less tangible than cold, hard cash. Perhaps for this reason, the waitress tends to treat jobs performed for the benefit of management as charitable deeds and to anticipate compensation for her helpfulness. If she agrees to pick up an unpromising party or cover for a co-worker who has "called out," she may insist on special consideration in seating or scheduling, or request assistance from management in bussing her tables. If assistance is not immediately forthcoming, she hints that in future she will be less generous with her favors, and she is likely to hold to her word.

In deed if not in word the manager supports the view that waitresses are not bound by his authority. This is suggested by the hesitance with which he makes requests of waitresses—to stay late, to pick up poor prospects—and by his tendency to abstain from reprimanding waitresses for failing to comply with company regulations. The manager's reluctance to issue orders and express criticism to the waitress is not solely a product of her financial independence, however. In his dealings with dishwashers and cooks as well as waitresses, the manager is constrained by a set of responsibilities, which more than any other aspect of his position, exemplifies the degradation of the managerial role.

Responsibilities of Manager as Fill-in Man

In discussing the possibility of advancement, employees inevitably express concern over the increased responsibility that would accompany a promotion to the managerial ranks. Such a concern is somewhat paradoxical since responsibility is typically heralded as a benefit, not a liability of upward progression. "Your internship will add greatly to your ability to assume a responsible management position" promises a brochure on a local management-training program distributed at the restaurant in an effort to stimulate interest in managerial careers. As used here, *responsibility* conjures images of authority and trust: a responsible manager is in control, in charge. The same positive understanding is implied in the advice of popular success manuals which counsel readers, "Always take the initiative in assuming greater responsibility. When you have demonstrated that you can deliver positive results . . . your supervisors will naturally give you even more responsibility" (Green 1989:227).[4]

The positive understanding of responsibility implied in company and popular usage is not shared within the Route organization. As defined by employees, managerial responsibility embodies two interrelated sets of duties, neither of which affords an opportunity to exercise authority or garner prestige. First, the manager is expected to compensate for absent employees with his own time and labor. Because the area around Route suffers from the double impact of rapid job growth and a severe shortage of labor, this duty necessarily absorbs a substantial portion, if not most of the manager's working hours. In itself, the prospect of circulating between the restaurant's six or seven job codes is not unappealing, particularly in an industry where prolonged tenure in any one job category can breed ennui. But the demand for managerial assistance is not equal in all work areas: turnover is disproportionately high among dishwashers, who also perform the majority of janitorial tasks in the restaurant, including vacuuming, mopping, taking out the garbage, and cleaning and stocking the bathrooms.

In an ongoing struggle to stay the flow of workers through the dish room, managers solicit the labor of those whose lack of options might motivate them to endure a job that has little else to offer other than its availability. Their efforts are in vain. The homeless men who are occasionally persuaded to exchange their posts on the benches of an adjacent parking lot for a position at the dish machine rarely return to repeat the experience. "Even our Work Release people," the general manager pointed out, "which are prisoners, they theirselves have a choice if they want to work or not work. . . . They don't want to work." In one instance, a prisoner released to the restaurant as part of the work program reportedly abandoned his dishwashing duties midshift, never to return to the restaurant or the prison. At different times the restaurant has also hired Jamaican, Ethiopian, Spanish, Mexican, and Chinese dishwashers, many of whom have minimal English language skills and might have difficulty finding employment elsewhere even during a labor crisis. Yet these workers quickly move on as well, and management is left to fill in the gaps. So frequently in fact does the disappearance of dishwashers necessitate a managerial substitute that promotion to management is often equated with consignation to the dish room. The resulting disparity between images of management as superordinate, responsible in the positive sense, and managerial responsibility as perceived by employees, is embodied in the common spectacle of the manager in a suit, with a tie, pulling bus pans, emptying garbage, sorting silverware.[5]

Understaffing is also a chronic problem on the line and on the floor, but the technical knowledge and speed required to function effectively in these areas make it difficult for managers to fill in as cooks and waitresses.[6] The manager's second responsibility therefore consists in alleviating the workload of these employees by acting as a backup in stress situations. When cooks are twenty-deep in checks, managers are enlisted to flip burgers, drop chicken, and man the microwaves.[7] When waitresses are "swamped," managers are commissioned to deliver drinks and make desserts. When salad, soda, ice, or ice cream runs low, managers are dispatched to the walk-in refrigerator, the stockroom, the storeroom, or the freezer. Above all, managers serve as backup for waitresses by acting as makeshift hostesses or assisting the hostess if one is on duty. Elegant title aside, hostesses do little more than run errands for waitresses. They are responsible for ringing up checks for departing parties, delivering to the appropriate server gratuities added to credit charges or left as change at the register. They also seat, "water," and distribute menus to incoming customers, maintaining a waiting list if there is a crowd at the door. It is here that the hostess's greatest difficulties lie.

In order for the hostess to seat customers, she must first locate a clean table. Waitresses are frequently too busy to bus a table when it is needed and are inclined to leave tables dirty to avoid being sat if they are behind, if they are trying to work off the floor, or if a party waiting to be seated is disagreeably large, unruly, or otherwise undesirable.[8] Consequently, the hostess—or manager— is often compelled to bus for the waitresses, simply to keep the line at the door moving. A manager who is acting as hostess may suggest that a waitress clear a particular table, but she is likely to respond by assuring him she will get to it, as she races by on her way to or from a party, knowing that he will soon break down under the impatient scrutiny of customers waiting to be seated, and clear the table himself. If the manager is more direct in his request, he is liable to provoke a more direct response.

> If [the manager] tells me, "Millie, you know, I need that table back there," while my whole entire station is full and there's one dirty table and my food is up and what not, or if I have to take an order, he's going to tell me—that aggravates the Hell out of me. He's going to tell me that he *needs* that table? And I just tell him, "Mr. Hollinger, if you need that table, you know what you can do with it."

The manager's duties as fill-in man and backup boy compromise his ability and willingness to uphold company policies he receives from higher-ups. Reluctant to spend his workday washing dishes and bussing tables, the manager hesitates to fire, rebuke, or in any manner precipitate the departure of employees. Aware of this reluctance, employees arrive for work late or not at all, indulge in frequent and flagrant violations of company policy, and neglect the less agreeable aspects of their work. Asked why the manager did not insist that the cooks fulfill their cleaning duties (*pulling the mats,* sweeping and mopping the line, scrubbing the grills, wiping down the walls, changing and stocking food inserts, changing the fryers), a cook explained:

> They have a hard enough time keeping cooks as it was so they didn't want to rock the boat and tell

them you got to do it. . . . They did [occasionally ask cooks to clean] and the cooks would laugh at them cause they knew that management wouldn't do anything if they didn't do the cleaning anyway.

Employee expectations of impunity in these cases are upheld by experience. Waitresses often recounted incidents in which transgressions of restaurant rules had gone uncensured by managers who felt that unreliable, dissident, and dishonest employees were better than none at all. With regard to management's tolerance of chronic tardiness and call-outs one waitress recalled:

> I'd be scheduled for three, four nights, and I might show up for two. But I wouldn't show up on time. . . . Not "boo" was said to me. Not "boo."

In reference to another waitress she commented:

> She was hired two months ago, and I think she's worked two days and called out and had a no-call, no-show ever since. They still haven't fired her. She comes in once every three weeks, one day. . . . I don't think the management has power over anyone. I don't think they control any of the workers. . . . Managers are afraid of using their authority, in any way, shape, and form.

As might be expected, the failure of managers to reprimand employees for violations of restaurant policy conduces to continued delinquency and compromises the credibility of management in the eyes of employees. Asked why she does not respect the management team at the restaurant, the waitress quoted above responded:

I'd respect them if they would have fired me. I don't respect them cause they don't. They should have fired me a long time ago. For calling out sick . . . for the amount of times I'm late. . . . It's stupidity on their part. . . . Hank [a waiter] got hired back after being fired for stealing money. . . . How are you supposed to respect someone, your boss . . . when they give you nothing to respect? If you fired me, fine, I would respect you. At least you stood your ground.

Another waitress commented in more general terms:

As far as management, I don't have any respect for them. . . . They don't know their sense of authority. They don't know how to show their authority to their employees. In other words, they let the employees run the store.

If they are to gain the respect and compliance of their staff, managers must impose negative sanctions on delinquent employees. Yet, by flexing their disciplinary muscle, managers increase the odds that they will spend their work hours filling in as cooks, hostesses, and especially dishwashers. The assumption of these roles, though considered obligatory by employees, helps to undercut employee respect for the managerial role, which increasingly comes to be seen as a menial job for menial workers.

Consequences of the Disparity between Image and Reality

Three factors limiting managerial authority have been examined: (1) the centralization of the decision-making function at higher levels in the organizational hierarchy, which reduces managers to mere "servants of decisions" handed down from above; (2) the tipping system, which transfers control over the waitress's income to the public thereby divesting managers of a traditional source and symbol of authority; and (3) the manager's responsibilities as fill-in man, which make him reluctant to fire, suspend, reprimand, or otherwise motivate the departure of employees, and which cause the managerial role to be associated with the performance of menial tasks. The position of manager as affected by these factors contrasts sharply with traditional images of management as a position of power and prestige. This disparity between image and reality has consequences for how the manager perceives his position within the organizational hierarchy and for the depth of his commitment to the managerial role; for management–employee relations, which affect the effective functioning of the restaurant; and finally, for how employees evaluate management as a prospective career. The final consequence is the topic of Chapter 5; the first two, implications for managerial self-perception and commitment and effects on management–employee relations, are discussed next.

Implications for Managerial Self-Perception and Commitment

The disjuncture between image and the reality of the managerial role is recognized by managers themselves who attribute high drop-out rates among new managers and managers-in-training to the disparity between expectations of having control and the experience of serving as backup boys and fill-in men. Mr. Innes, a manager with the company for ten years, attributes the disparity between expectation and experience to unrealistic aspirations acquired in college, which are later reinforced by the company's management-training program.

> A lot of newcomers come in, they don't stay too long. Because it's not what they expect. . . . They're trained in a unit where it's the ideal situation. . . . You got four cooks, you got three dishwashers, you got seven waitresses on the floor, you got a hostess. . . . And when they come into the real world, it's not there. . . . They find out . . . they have to go pull off their jacket, go back in the kitchen and cook, or . . . go back and wash dishes. They're not going to put up with that. . . . [As college students], they see going in, walking around, you know as a supervisor, with a suit on. . . . They don't see taking their coat off, going in the dish room, or having to go and cook. They don't visualize that.

Similarly, the general manager credits the company with instilling unrealistic expectations of the managerial career when attempting to promote employees from within.

> They go ahead and paint a rosy picture. They don't explain to them about all the problems you're going to have. . . . Let's say a waitress, a cook, or even a dishwasher, they've proved theirselves to be excellent employees and go into management. A waitress . . . can make about . . . four hundred dollars a week take-home. . . . A few months down the road they realize that their managers are not even taking that much home. They're putting in more hours, more aggravation, and more stress. The result is they go back to

being a waitress, or a cook, or a dishwasher. In the beginning they feel that [being a manager has] got prestige, it's powerful, they're managers and they're going to be delegating. But then they'll find out for example . . . come eleven o'clock you have no graveyard help, you just cannot pack up and leave. . . . You as the manager are responsible for this store. So what you're going to have to do is stay all night. Either pick up, cook, or do dishes, cause you're understaffed.

Given the essentially negative views of the management role conveyed in these comments, it is difficult to understand why managers continue to "put up with" the trials of their position. While tact did not permit posing the question, two of the three full-time managers interviewed volunteered the information that they regarded their current jobs as temporary: stepping-stones to careers outside the company. One manager explained that he was only working at the restaurant so he could be close to his mother (who was ill) and familiarize himself with the area's hotel industry. Another explained that he planned to open a restaurant of his own and saw his present job as preparation for that goal: "I have a book [in which] I note the mistakes they make. . . . When I go into business for myself, I won't make the same mistakes. . . . So actually what I'm doing, I'm getting experience to go in business for myself at someone else's expense." A third manager, who eventually left the company to drive a poultry truck (this shortly after being promoted to general manager and receiving his own Route store), harbored dreams of opening a wholesale seafood business on the West Coast. So, while many prospective managers withdraw physically from the managerial role when confronted with the disjuncture between expectation and experience, others seek refuge from the frustration of disillusionment in dreams of moving up by getting out.

Withdrawal from the managerial role may be precipitated by feelings of ambivalence and anxiety concerning the manager's position in the larger organizational structure. Like the marginalized and disempowered foreman, the restaurant manager is apt to feel that he is technically part of the company's managerial stratum but functionally a rank-and-file employee. The manager's ambivalence concerning his status is expressed in his inclination to alternate between speaking of the company in the first and third person: as *we* or as *they, the company,* and *Route.* In referring to Route in the first person plural, the manager identifies himself as an integral part of the company. In using the third person, he distances himself from Route and conceptually divorces his own interests and actions from those of the company.

The manager's uncertainty concerning his status is clearly expressed in instances in which he switches midsentence between speaking in the first and third person, as in the following comments of Mr. Innes:

> The hours that [waitresses] want to work, it doesn't really suit our—the needs of the business.

> Route they—we pay 100 percent.

Significantly, Innes used *we* primarily when discussing problems related specifically to his unit, but switched to *they* when speaking of policies of the company as a whole. In reference to cost and labor problems of his own restaurant, Innes commented:

Labor, employee morale, food costs—all the costs is a problem that we have to contend with.

Get to the point we couldn't get anybody from the unemployment office.

But in reference to the company's medical coverage he remarked:

The company pay 80 percent of the major medical insurance. The other 20 percent you have to pay yourself, or you have another insurance company. . . . Route Company . . . they pay 80 percent.

And in reference to the company's management-training program, Innes said:

They modify it since then. To be honest I really don't know exactly what they do. What they doing now is they taking a manager after he went through the phase as an employee and put them in a real-life situation.

Here, Mr. Innes acknowledges his marginalization from policy formation concerning the training of new managers implicitly by speaking in the third person and explicitly, by conceding his ignorance of current procedures. Innes's general inclination to say *we* when referring to negative matters affecting his unit specifically, while using *they* when discussing neutral or positive policies affecting the entire company, suggests that he feels accountable for problems that arise within his store but does not feel involved in the setting of broader and potentially constructive policies. Because Innes has worked with Route Restaurant for ten years it is unlikely that his uncertainty concerning his status is a transitory symptom of settling into the management role. Rather, status anxiety appears to be a chronic affliction associated with the manager's position.

Mr. Watts, a manager who had worked at Routes in Florida, Pennsylvania, and in other areas of New Jersey before being transferred to his present post, expressed his understanding of the company hierarchy and his position within it in unusually explicit terms. In discussing his work, Watts often alluded cynically to the setting of policies by "California." When asked whether he was responsible for the recent installation of fluorescent lights in the restaurant, he responded:

> No. Somebody in California Route and now they're putting them in all Routes. I knew that [fluorescent lights save money and give off more light] six years ago, you know. If I would have suggested them, if I went to Garrison [the district manager] and suggested them, he'd look at me like some kind of nut.

Shortly afterward, Watts commented that he had no opportunity to innovate in his present position "because California makes all the decisions." In a different context, he remarked:

> I would love to sit down with the man [the district manager] and discuss things. I really would. Because I have some fantastic ideas. Cause you can go through the politics of bringing it to California's attention and California examining it and going along and him getting a nice little star.

These remarks reveal Mr. Watts's awareness of the extreme centralization that characterizes Route and of the counterproductive consequences of centralization: a manager who comes up with an idea to save the company money will be seen as a "nut"—not, presumably, because the idea is absurd—but because having an idea is absurd. Moreover, to get a "fantastic" idea heard requires that one engage in a political maneuver. Watts's final comment is significant on two counts. First, it reveals his recognition of the degraded status of management within the organization. A manager two levels above him will be rewarded for his efforts after the fashion of a second grader, with "a nice little star." His contribution will not be rewarded by increased pay or a louder voice in shaping company policy in the future. Second, the assumption that the district manager would receive a reward for his ideas reveals Watts's sense of personal insignificance as one whose voice, if heard at all, must be attributed to another.

Consequences for Management–Employee Relations

The managers' uncertainty over their organizational status engenders ambivalence toward their role as fill-in men, which, above all else, symbolizes the decline of managerial authority. From their comments concerning the high turnover rates among new managers and managers-in-training it is clear that Route managers acknowledge the role of fill-in as an integral component of managerial responsibility. Managers do not say that they sometimes choose to help out on the line or in the dish room; they say that as managers they "have to . . . go back in the kitchen and cook, or . . . go back and wash dishes." Still, managers do not fully embrace the role of fill-in man. They allude wistfully to managers of other restaurants who sit in the office and do paper work all day. Occasionally they also attempt to resist pressures to serve as fill-in men, by retreating to the office during a rush, or by insisting on the urgency of paper work when wait-resses signal for assistance. That managers are not fully reconciled to the fill-in role is further reflected in their oblique appeals for gratitude (recurrent references to hours worked, jobs performed, fatigue suffered) from employees who have benefited from their assistance, and in the muttered complaints with which they carry out their round of petty tasks. The extent to which managers may resent the responsibilities of fill-in man is suggested by Mr. Watts's comments concerning a period of several weeks during which he was forced to wait tables full time: "Man that hurt. You don't know. It was like stripping me of my clothes and making me walk out in front of every-body naked."

In contrast to managers, employees make no dis-tinction between what is and what should be with respect to the managerial position. Though they acknowledge that the managerial role is overburdened with respon-sibility, they expect those who accept the role to bear the burden in full. For managers to protest the fulfillment of responsibilities they have agreed to accept, is perceived as laziness and cause for contempt. Accordingly, wait-resses respond to managers' calls for sympathy with de-termined indifference: a stiff shrug, a counterreference to their own exertions, or silence. The ensuing lack of sym-pathy between "lazy" managers and "thankless" employ-ees inspires a cycle of retaliatory recalcitrance in which each side calibrates its work exertions so as not to exceed the effort of the other. Unappreciated for their assump-tion of responsibilities they do not fully accept, managers continue to resist and sometimes reject employee requests for aid. To employees, such rejection constitutes neglect of job duties and grounds for reciprocal negligence. Thus, employees invoke the failure of managers to "do more" as they engage in myriad acts of petty dissidence: sidework is neglected, schedules misinterpreted, phones within arm's reach go unheard.

One part-time manager, known for his heroic feats of hard work, explained the employee response as follows:[9]

> You [as a manager] don't command respect, you have to earn it. I mean maybe years ago that was the way it was but in today's environment, that's not the way it is. . . . You don't go up to tell someone just to do this, do that. You've got to earn respect from the people. . . . And believe me, you'll get the respect from your employees by working. . . .
>
> When people see that a manager is giving his 110 percent, people are going to do the same thing. . . . If people see that the manager is going . . . to sit on his ass and do nothing . . . they're going to say, "Well what the Hell should *I* work for?"

Through his readiness to work the longest shifts, perform the dirtiest work (unclogging toilets, killing roaches), and help everyone all the time, this manager had established exceptional rapport with the restaurant's employees. The failure of other managers to give 110 percent, and fulfill their obligations as fill-in men, weakened their relations with the staff and in some cases precipitated the departure, temporary or permanent, of aggravated workers. One waitress of six years gave notice (scribbled angrily on the back of a napkin), following a manager's failure to

greet her customers properly or provide them with water—duties she perceived as falling within the realm of
managerial responsibility.

These findings provide support for the hypothesis
that the position of manager may no longer be desired or
necessarily desirable. Such a possibility suggests in turn
that the rejection of advancement by waitresses and other
low-ranking employees may be provoked by the shortcomings of higher-level jobs, and not of the workers who
reject them. Before exploring this hypothesis it will be
necessary to examine the character and quality of the
waitress's work life more closely: to determine whether
she has something to lose as well as nothing to gain by
ascending the occupational ladder.

4

Sources of Autonomy

In order to ensure management control and to cheapen the worker, conception and execution must be rendered separate spheres of work, and for this purpose the study of work processes must be reserved to management and kept from the workers, to whom its results are communicated only in the form of simplified job tasks governed by simplified instructions which it is thenceforth their duty to follow unthinkingly and without comprehension of the underlying technical reasoning or data.

—*Harry Braverman,* Labor and Monopoly Capital

I'm so relaxed at Route because . . . when I come in there, it's what I want to do, regardless of what you say, you know. Like, "Don't tell me nothing. I know what I got to do."

—*Route waitress*

At Route each detail of service delivery is meticulously regulated by company specifications or *SPECs*. SPECs instruct a waitress how to unwrap a straw and how to be friendly in terms equally specific, equally explicit. SPECs tell the waitress how many croutons to put on a salad; how many ounces of hot fudge to ladle over how many ounces of what kind of ice cream in preparing a sundae; how much ice to put in soft drinks; how to say hello; whether it is more important to finish taking an order or pick up an order; when and how often to check on customers after the entree is served; and when and how to clear dirty plates off the table. SPECs also tell her how long her hair will hang, how long her earrings will dangle, on which side of her uniform she will pin her name tag, what color hose she will wear, and whether she will have stripes on her dark-brown shoes.

In spite of this extensive system of regulations, waitresses enjoy considerable autonomy, or freedom from external constraint (Katz 1968), in their work lives. They control many of the decisions relating to the management of their stations and parties; they regulate the tempo of their work and the volume of business they do; they compromise dress code; and they eat and rest when it suits them—all without interference from management or co-workers. It has already been suggested that as tipped employees, waitresses operate beyond the range of managerial control. Other factors that contribute to their autonomy include the inadequate training they receive as rookies; the restaurant's climate of chaos; the irregular pace and the structuring of waitressing work; high turnover rates among managers; the manager's role as fill-in man; and the labor crisis.

Sources of Autonomy

Inadequate Training

To help the new waitress learn SPECs, the company has recently developed an elaborate training package, complete with glossy flash cards, bulleted summaries, workbooks, and quizzes. In addition, the company distributes training videos that review SPECs and demonstrate effective strategies for handling disgruntled or cantankerous customers. In one video, a seasoned veteran imparts company-sanctioned waitressing strategies to a rookie as they stroll through the park on their day off. The tactics suggested by the veteran are vague and obvious: a waitress should use her time wisely; she should coordinate tasks to avoid extra trips; she should be cheerful. Still, after the meeting the rookie is thankful, enlightened, and eager to put her newfound knowledge to the test.

In reality few waitresses ever see the training videos, or know a formal training system with flash cards, workbooks, and quizzes exists. There are two reasons for this. First, managers have difficulty persuading experienced waitresses to act as trainers. Waitresses are unwilling to come in on their days off to train for four dollars an hour when they are accustomed to making over ten, and are reluctant to be "shadowed" during a shift since trainees tend to get in the way (their own and their co-workers') and slow the trainer down. Second, rookies are inevitably compelled to start waiting tables on their own after a few days or hours of preparation to compensate for call-outs and no-shows. A waitress's recollection of her first days at the restaurant frequently begins with a reference to the insufficient training she received.

> My experience at Route was [pause] easy. I went through no training. They just threw me on the floor.

In reference to her first waitressing experience at a different restaurant another waitress commented:

> It was a madhouse. . . . I never waitressed in my life before . . . [and] they just threw me to the

wolves. They fed me to the wolves. They kicked me out on the floor. It was like, "You're on your own, kid."

To be *thrown on the floor* is standard waitress terminology for being forced to wait tables before one is adequately trained. The violence of the expression and the fact that such an expression exists reveal that the experience is both traumatic and common.

Because they are *thrown on the floor,* most waitresses are never exposed to the carefully researched and standardized procedures prescribed by the company. They learn to survive on the floor, not by recourse to policies they never learned, but by watching fellow employees and by improvising. As a result, waitresses develop individualized work habits which often diverge significantly from SPECs. How desserts are made, how orders are taken, how codes are written, which bowl is used to serve soup or salad, even the price of certain menu items, vary depending on the waitress. She bases her decisions on her sense of what is most efficient or pleasing to the customer and most compatible with her personal abilities and inclinations. Once her work patterns are established, managers do not interfere to change them. They are often ignorant of the proper procedures themselves and cannot, in any case, feel justified criticizing employees for failing to adhere to policies they were not given a chance to learn. Waitresses seem to understand this; at least, they never entirely forget—or let their managers forget—that they were thrown on the floor and denied guidance when they needed it most.

The Contribution of Chaos

A second factor that undermines company efforts to regularize, or "rationalize," the delivery of service is the inherently frenzied nature of restaurant work. Chronic shortages of labor and supplies converge with unpredictable peaks in demand to create a context of chaos in which waitresses are forced to override company specifications to get their work accomplished. At the height of a rush, when the dishwasher is dwarfed by a mountain of bus pans and every low-a-lator is empty, the waitress is compelled to serve salad dressing in teapots and toast in soup bowls.[1] She dilutes the chicken soup to two-thirds water to eke out one last bowl and fabricates a price for popcorn shrimp rather than waste time hunting through the off-menu price list. Managers encourage the waitress's use of ad hoc solutions by employing creative problem solving themselves, and by responding to pleas for help with exasperation or not at all. For the waitress, the freedom to innovate during crisis periods, like the enforced independence of the rookie, is a burden rather than a privilege. Every trip to an empty low-a-lator, every dash at an empty silver bin, every watery bowl of soup decreases the speed and quality of her service and ultimately detracts from her tip earnings. What is resented as lack of support in one context, however, is claimed as a right to autonomy in others. Forced to seek creative solutions during stress periods, the waitress assumes the right to control the decisions of her work during periods of relative tranquility and abundance. This applies particularly with respect to dress code.

> You're [management] going to sit here and yap at me because my earrings hang an inch too long . . . or maybe I have one hair out of place, or I have fingernail polish on? Over everything in the store, where I have no silverware, no glasses, and so forth, you're going to give me a half an hour lecture on fingernail polish?[2]

In addition to fingernail polish and conspicuous jewelry, some workers wear gleaming white tennis shoes, others leave their hair down, regularly misplace their name tags, or launder them with their uniforms until they are illegible.

The failure of managers to provide adequate support staff, and above all, dishwashers to whom employees can communicate their needs, provides waitresses with additional grounds for noncompliance. One waitress, known for letting her slip show and leaving the back of her shirt untucked (though she dressed immaculately during off hours and at her other job), justified her persistent slovenliness to the district manager as follows:

> I said [to the district manager], "We're working with people that don't even speak English. Let alone you want me to come in here looking all prim and proper. Uh-uh. Doesn't work like that. We have busboys that don't even know yes and no . . . and you want me to 'yes, yes' and be all nice, and with a slip up?" And I said, "Ah. It don't work like that."

The implicit logic reads that if the company fails to meet its obligation to maintain favorable working conditions, the waitress in turn is not obliged to fulfill her responsibility to meet company dress standards.

Customers contribute to the chaotic nature of restaurant work and help thwart efforts to rationalize service by introducing an uncontrollable degree of irregularity into the service process. They invariably request the unexpected, reject what they are supposed to demand, arrive when they should be leaving, and stay when they should go. They are the ultimate wild card that ensures that service industries will never become smoothly regulated, steadily ticking factories; and that waitresses will never become mere cogs in a service machine. As long as it is the waitress's job to minister to the unpredictable needs and tastes of her parties, she will need to innovate, to evaluate, to order and reorder priorities—to think.

Irregular Pace of Restaurant Work

The pace of the waitress's work is not determined by the speed of a conveyor belt or the rhythm of a machine, but by the inherently irregular flow of customers through the restaurant. At Route, weekends and certain times of the day (midmorning and midevening for instance) tend to be busy, while others (early morning and late afternoon) are generally slow; but there are always surprises. A snowstorm can create a sudden drop in business; the unannounced arrival of a bus of basketball players can cause a storm of activity on the floor and in the kitchen. On busy shifts and during rushes, the waitress runs to keep pace with her parties and does not have time to pull up her nylons between waiting tables or wipe the whipped cream out of her hair. But on moderate or slow shifts, during lulls in business, and whenever she has spare time between taking and delivering orders, she is free to talk, eat, rest, wander, smoke cigarettes, and drink coffee. Grave workers are especially likely to have empty time on their hands, and they make use of it very much as they please. One waitress recalled:

> I used to bring homework there and do it, bring my typewriter and type term papers. . . . Gwen [a co-waitress] and I used to take turns. . . . While one's sleeping, the other one's on the floor. . . . While Gwen's sleeping, I be doing my

homework or something, and I wait on the customers. . . . I read one paragraph, go wait on a table, put their order in, come back and finish reading the rest of it.

Managers rarely attempt to coax workers on graveyard or on other shifts to utilize quiet periods productively, and workers make no effort to simulate productiveness when managers approach. Now and then one Route manager glowered at employees who were reading papers and smoking cigarettes while he was still stuck cooking or seating customers, but his glowering was not succeeded by any more direct form of criticism and was largely ignored.

Here as elsewhere, the waitress's impunity from managerial interference can be attributed to her independence as a tipped employee and to the manager's hesitance to risk aggravating workers. Waitresses and managers may also be engaged in an implicit exchange of interests, in which waitresses waive their right to formal breaks, and managers do not censure them for relaxing on the job. Though workers are entitled to a half hour for meals on eight-hour shifts, only dishwashers, some cooks, and rookie servers ever request formal time off. Except when working double shifts, waitresses never mention the possibility of taking a break, preferring to rest intermittently throughout the course of a shift. This arrangement benefits management, which does not have to worry about covering for waitresses on break; and waitresses, who do not lose tips while they rest, and enjoy the satisfaction of being able to structure their work time as they see fit. Comparing Route's work rhythm to her job as a directory assistance operator at New Jersey Bell, one waitress said:

I have a lot of freedom at Route. At the [New Jersey Bell job] I'm so confined, there's so much stress at this job. Girl, it's a heartache! To the point where it's like military. You have a certain time you supposed to take a break, then when you supposed to be back there, you have to be there on time, on time, all the time.

For workers accustomed to the rigid timetable of more structured jobs, the prospect of taking a scheduled break and having to be back "on time, all the time," would seem neither strange nor unusually demanding. But the waitress is accustomed to deciding for herself whether she can and needs to rest and regards this kind of "military" control as uncomfortably restricting.

Structuring of the Waitress's Work

Route waitresses are not interdependent units in an integrated work process, but independent workers performing parallel tasks. Each waitress is assigned an approximately equal number of tables and booths which serves as her station for the duration of her shift. In some cases her station may be partially closed off from those of her co-workers. She may have her own counter, her own silver bins, coffeepots, and bus pans, and even a door that she can close when she no longer wishes to take parties. Unless there is a hostess or manager running the front house, the waitress tends to most of her customers' needs herself. She sets the table in preparation for incoming parties; "waters" customers while they wait to order; takes the order; makes salads, portions soup, rolls, and other extras; prepares beverages; picks up and delivers the main order; makes all desserts; prices, adds, taxes, and delivers the check; then clears and resets the table for the next party.[3] Often the waitress also seats her own parties and "rings them up" on their way out. During all this, she may cross paths and exchange comments with other servers, but there is no coordination of tasks, no division of labor among waitresses.

To some extent waitress and cook are interdependent workers, and each must monitor her or his work performance so as not to impede the effective functioning of the other. Cooks should not *put up* three of the waitress's orders at once or prepare entrees before appetizers; waitresses should not let food get cold in the cooks' window so that it needs to be recooked, or put five checks on the wheel simultaneously.[4] Apart from these exercises in courtesy, the waitress does not need to regulate the tempo or decisions of her work to correspond to the expectations or speed of other workers. She may choose to take the order for a large party after she has picked up several two-tops, or she may pick up the big party first.[5] She may decide to let the man at the counter who stiffed her last Saturday sit twenty minutes before taking his order. She may opt to take all the drink orders in her station before taking any meal orders. If she is tired or backed up, she can slow the movement of customers into her station by ignoring parties at the door or by leaving her tables dirty; if she is anxious to maximize her tip earnings, she can employ any of the usual tactics for increasing customer count (discussed in Chapter 2). In each case, her decision affects only her and her customers and is hers to make, without consulting or striving to accommodate co-workers or management.

In this respect, waitresses enjoy greater freedom in the performance of their work than managers or other restaurant workers. As we have seen, the manager is forever at the beck and call of employees who expect him to alleviate their workload in pressure situations. Dish-washers and cooks meanwhile work as teams (when more than one is on duty), and each member must synchronize his activities to conform to the work patterns of the group. In the dish room one worker runs the dish machine, while another pulls bus pans and stocks supplies. In the kitchen, each cook tends a different part of the line (for example, grills, fryers), and the most experienced cook *calls the wheel.* Specifically, this means that the lead cook pulls checks down from the wheel, interprets the wait-resses' ordering codes, and calls out to the other cooks what is needed for a given group of orders. He also acts as the primary mediator between the line and the floor and is responsible for preparing certain parts of the orders (for example, eggs, omelettes, toast, pancakes). In this divi-sion of labor, each cook contributes a different item to a single plate and must keep pace with the cook calling the wheel and with his co-workers, much as auto workers must keep pace with the assembly line. In contrast, wait-resses work by themselves, for themselves.

Finally, it should be noted that the waitress's work does not lend itself easily to close supervision. Even if managers were inclined to interfere with the waitress's work patterns and were not already busy washing dishes or cooking, they could not simultaneously keep track of each server as she raced between tables, kitchen, and stockroom on a thousand ever-changing missions. Nor could they monitor the waitress's interaction with her customers, since most of this takes place on the floor, out of earshot of management, and is in a sense private. Managers and co-waitresses cannot comfortably inter-rupt or even approach a waitress while she is "at a table": customers appear to consider such interruptions rude, and on this point the waitress agrees.

> At Happy's [another restaurant] I got so annoyed
> after a while, that if the manager came up to me
> and disturbed me while I was taking an order—
> which I *loathe*—I hate it when people do that
> cause it's my time with the customer, not my
> time, the customer's time, and the manager's
> time—I would just turn around and yell at him on
> the floor, you know, "I'll get it later!"

In the privacy of her station, the waitress can be cheerful
or cold to her customers as she deems appropriate; she
can neglect to introduce herself to her parties though she
is directed to do so by SPECs; and she can mislead
customers concerning the price, preparation, or progress
of their orders, confident that no one is listening over her
shoulder.

Managerial Turnover

High turnover rates at the managerial level contribute to the waitress's autonomy by handicapping managers with perpetual rookie status. A waitress who works
at Route for six years may see twelve or more managers
pass through her store, and three or more district managers pass through her district. Managers, like waitresses, are liable to be "fed to the wolves" before they are
fully trained, and a new manager is likely to find himself
alone in a store, unfamiliar with the staff, uncertain of the
physical setup, confronted with a crowd of impatient
customers as well as a shortage of dishwashers, cooks,
waitresses, and supplies. Particularly if he is new to the
company, the incoming manager will rely on senior waitresses to keep order in the front house: to seat, take extra
parties, and reorganize stations when the inevitable call-
outs come in. Once this pattern of dependency is established it is not easily reversed. Managers cannot feel

comfortable issuing orders to and correcting the procedure of waitresses who led them by the hand weeks
earlier. Moreover, waitresses come to expect autonomy
and regard the prospect of intervention by transient managers with contempt.

> I'm so relaxed at Route because . . . when I come
> in there, it's what I want to do, regardless of what
> you say, you know. Like, "Don't tell me nothing.
> I know what I got to do." That's just like how I am
> there cause I been there so long. How you going
> to tell me what to do? I been there this, this, this,
> and this long and you going to come in and you
> just getting here trying to tell me what to do?
> Child, please.[6]

The waitress does not hesitate to challenge the
authority or criticize the conduct of the manager or district manager, particularly if he attempts to alter her work
patterns. The following incident took place at Andy's
Restaurant and is recalled by a waitress who now works at
Route:

> I had every Tuesday and Saturday off . . . and he
> [a new manager] had scheduled me for *both* of
> those days. And . . . I went into the office and I
> started yelling at him. I said, "I *always* have Tues-
> day and Saturday off. Who are you to come in
> here and start changing my schedule around?"
> And he said to me, "If you're the headwaitress,
> then you can work any day, any shift I want you to
> work." "Well," I said, "well then I don't need it."

Another waitress recalled her response to the district
manager's cancellation of her health insurance (for which

she no longer qualified) prior to an inspection by his boss, the regional manager:

> I said [to the district manager], "Your boss comes in and all of a sudden you feel like going through files and doing paper work?" . . . And he goes, "Oh, oh, Meryl. . . . You are absolutely right. It was very unprofessional of me. And I, I apologize. I am very sorry." I said, "Apologize? You did it unprofessional. I signed no papers. . . ." I just blew up at him. . . . "Listen, you did something wrong. I know what I'm doing. I been there for nine years, so you're not getting over on me."

In recounting the incident, the waitress acknowledged that she was ineligible for Route benefits, since she did not work the required thirty hours a week, and that she was in any case receiving benefits from her second job with the state. She claimed to be angry only because the district manager's failure to notify her prior to dropping her insurance was "unprofessional." Even so, it may be inferred that her anger arose in part from a sense that as a relative newcomer, the district manager should not have interfered with the established order of the restaurant—however much this order conflicted with company policy.

The Vulnerability of Management and the Labor Crisis

We saw earlier that the manager's responsibilities as fill-in man place him in a position in which he is unwilling to impose negative sanctions, and that employees take advantage of this reluctance to compromise restaurant rules, most notably with respect to work attendance. Employees also exploit the manager's vulnerability as fill-in man directly, to increase their control and resist interference in their work lives. Between managers and senior employees, and especially experienced waitresses, virtually all negotiation takes the form of an ultimatum: management must comply with the employee's demands or redress her grievance, or she will leave. So often does a cook threaten to walk off the line or a waitress threaten to walk off the floor, that the act has acquired an almost ritual consistency. In the following instance, a waitress who was angered that a co-waitress was staying late and potentially "tapping into" her money, ensured that she would be favorably "seated," despite the extra person on the floor, by threatening to walk out.

> I said, "Innes, I'm in [station] one and two. If one and two is not filled at all times from now until three, I'm getting my coat, my pocketbook, and *I'm leaving*." And one and two was filled, and I made ninety-five dollars. (emphasis added)

A pregnant waitress threatened to leave unless the manager allowed her to wait tables in a sweatshirt.

> He gave me this extra, extra large [uniform], . . . then he made me work in a regular outfit. . . . I kind of resented to have to walk around in my typical Route uniform with this gut hanging out. . . . So I just told him, "I'm going off the floor. I'm buying a sweatshirt." So I had to run down to Acme, and I bought a sweatshirt with a lion on it. . . . I was working in that sweatshirt . . . or you weren't having me work. . . . I was like, "Either you compromise my way or *I'm leaving*." Simple as that. I will make a fool of myself for no one. (emphasis added)

A waitress may also threaten to quit permanently if her needs are not met.

> The reason why they changed me [from grave-yard to swing] was because I told them, I said, "You know what? . . . Either you take me off this shift, or I quit. Because I can't work this shift. My baby gets up when I get home. I can't sleep, because he's walking around doing this and that and then I woke up many a day when he had the flour all over the floor or the Vaseline rubbed all up against the T.V. and all on the wall and all up in my hair and on his hair and on his shirt". . . . And I said, "Either you change my hours, or *I'm leav-ing*." . . . But they changed my hours though, cause I sure was leaving. (emphasis added)

She may threaten to quit on a regular basis as a means of ensuring she will not be aggravated by managerial inter-ference.

> I saw Hollinger's expression when I told him I was going to get another job. . . . He gave me that clue right there that, "If you leave, I don't know what we're going to *do*" . . . and I grabbed that real fast. And I said, "Mr. Hollinger's afraid that I'm going to leave. I have him now where I want him. He won't give me any abuse." And he doesn't. I got him right here. Every time I say, "Well, Mr. Hollinger, on my last day here,"—he got all paranoid and . . . it's just like, "My God, she's leaving us." I have that on him. . . . I have him in a corner.

By threatening to walk off the floor or the line, or by threatening to quit, the waitress or cook signals to the manager that she is dissatisfied with some aspect of her work.[7] Generally the manager will take action to remedy the problem or, if this is not possible, will apologize to or voice sympathy with the aggrieved employee. Should a manager fail to rectify the problem or express appropriate concern, the employee's threat may be fulfilled, as in the following incident, which occurred at another Route unit.

> I blew up at the manager and can't remember what it was over. . . . We had three new girls on and they kept messing up. . . . I don't have any stock. The manager came over and started harassing me. I told her, "Get off my line. I don't want to see you back here again tonight, or I'm leaving." She left and came back and started in on me about something. I said, "*You* cook." Threw my apron at her and walked out the door.

As this cook throws the apron preparatory to walking off the line, a waitress typically throws her order book when walking off the floor.

> I was the only one on the floor and it was getting busy and Tess Martin [a co-waitress] was getting ready to go home and she says, "If you want any help, just yell." And smoking was filled and then nonsmoking started filling up. I was fine till I got a party of eight walk in on me. And Tess comes up front and I said, "I'm fine. Just leave me alone." And then she said something to me, and I went off on her. I threw my book in her face. I said,

> "Goodbye." I walked out the door. . . . Smoking was full. The counter was full. Half of nonsmoking was full. . . . I had checks in the window. Checks with food that had to come out.

In both cases the employee rids her(him)-self of a central symbol and instrument of the job, thereby signaling physically withdrawal from the work role. By throwing an apron or book at the manager or at a fellow employee, the waitress or cook also symbolizes the transfer of her duties to the recipient. In effect, she revenges herself against those who have provoked her anger by transferring her difficulties (a busy line or a crowded station) to the offender.

Although it is less common, workers may walk out in concert and effect a kind of impromptu strike. Because tension is highest when the restaurant is busy, such strikes are likely to occur when managers are most dependent upon their workers. One employee recalled a spontaneous strike, which took place at a different Route:

> One day something happened and the general manager got everybody ticked at him. He was left with, I think, one cook. Everybody walked off on him. He had three cooks in, he had three or four girls out on the floor. . . . One cook left, then another one left. A waitress got ticked at him and left before both the cooks. He was getting on everybody's nerves that day.

No threats of mass walkouts were carried out at the Kendelport store during the research period, but there is some evidence that such events have taken place in the past. Before coming to Route, I was employed as a waitress at Andy's, a nearby restaurant of similar style. One hectic Sunday morning Andy's was suddenly besieged by angry customers, who explained that the Route staff had just walked off the job, leaving no one to cook or serve their food. Strangely, waitresses at Route did not remember the incident when questioned about it several years later—an indication perhaps that the episode was not sufficiently novel to warrant remembrance.

Of course, waitresses would not feel so comfortable walking off the job and threatening to quit, and their threats would not have the same effect on management, if work were hard to find and employees were easily replaced. In the area in which Route is located, however, the labor shortage is so severe that other employers occasionally visit the restaurant in the guise of customers and attempt to poach workers. One waitress recalled how the manager of an expensive hotel and restaurant tried to lure away two of Route's most experienced full-time waitresses:

> This manager from [the hotel] came in [to the restaurant] and had offered Elise and Nera a job . . . and he was setting up an interview with me too. That's terrible . . . for a manager to be coming into another place and stealing all the help. And he was there for a long time, and he must of been like watching how we operate and whatnot.

Despite the disapproval she expresses for the manager's unethical methods, the waitress agreed to interview with the hotel. Another waitress accepted an offer to work as a desk clerk at a nearby motel, though she continued to work at Route also.

> I met this guy one night when I was working graveyard. He said, "Do you like Route's job?" I

said, "It's okay." He says, "Well I have a new motel. . . . Why don't you come down and we'll see about getting you a job where you don't have to work all night." So I said, "Okay."

At a time when employers must stoop to stealing workers from their competitors, employees can afford to be somewhat nonchalant about quitting—or being fired.

My attitude was always, when I was on graveyard, if they don't like what I do, if they find out that I eat a couple steaks a week, they can fire me. I'll go get another job. We're not stupid. We read the papers. We know there's a shortage of waiters and waitresses and cooks all over the world. They can fire me here. You know, I came here first for this reason or that. I'll very easily leave for any reason.

The labor shortage and the manager's vulnerability as fill-in man allow the worker to push the limits of her freedom, secure in the knowledge that she will not suffer the ultimate penalty as a consequence of her actions—or knowing, at least, that if she does, her unemployment will be short-lived. Put differently, these factors of her work environment minimize the risk factor in the strategies she employs to expand the boundaries of her autonomy.

Threats to Autonomy

Walking off the job, or threatening to do so, is an expression of autonomy in that it reflects the absence or weakness of hierarchical control. It is also a step typically taken when autonomy is threatened. In the following comments, a cook recalls his reaction to a manager's interference with his work when he was still a dishwasher:

> He [the manager] wouldn't listen. The dish machine was down. He was trying to tell me *I* had to use it. Doesn't work. It's got to sit for forty-five minutes or whatever time the chemical works. We were trying to do dishes by hand. Keep the place clean. Pull bus pans, get the stock out for the cooks and the waitresses. And *he's* trying to tell me this. And I was like, "It won't work." So he tried. He went over and started running the machine, and I went out the door. I walked right out the door and left him.

Though the manager might have saved the dishwasher the trouble of doing dishes manually, his intervention inspired anger, not gratitude. Similarly, in the following episode the interference of a manager engenders resentment despite the fact that the manager's actions would presumably benefit the employees concerned.

> [The manager] had busboys come out, bussing tables, bringing a bus pan to tables with people still sitting at them. Okay? And we were getting really upset, so Tess, Shelly, and I and Celina were going to get ready, I swear it, all four of us were going to go out the door and leave Meryl and Nera, man. . . . He was sitting people at tables . . . I mean, we'd just get them wiped and then . . . he would sit people there before

we even got silverware or anything to the tables. . . . Ken [a part-time manager] was there
and Ken knew we were all getting upset and mad
at him, man. . . . He said to [the manager] a
couple times, "You better watch what you're doing, because these girls are all getting upset."

It is not uncommon for managers, acting as hostesses, to bus tables in an effort to alleviate stress during a
rush. In this case, however, the waitresses were clearly
bombed out (overburdened with customers), and if left
alone would have let dirty tables sit long enough to catch
up with parties in progress. The manager's attempt to
accelerate the speed of service may have been motivated
by a desire to move more customers through the restaurant and increase revenues, by a concern for customer
satisfaction, or by an honest wish to help the waitresses.
It is conceivable also that the manager, who was sometimes accused of enjoying chaos, was striving to heighten
the clamor and confusion of an already hectic shift. Whatever his motivation, the manager's assistance was unso-
licited—or imposed—and regarded as unwanted and
unwarranted interference by most of the waitresses on
duty. Meryl and Nera, who are known as fast, efficient,
"money-hungry" waitresses, apparently did not plan to
take part in the walkout. It is probable that for them the
pecuniary benefits of accelerated service overrode the
negative implications of interference.

The potential for managerial interference to provoke ill will is illustrated in the next episode, which took
place at another Route following the manager's attempt to
assist a waitress by making a milk shake for one of her
customers. It was rumored at other Route units in the
area that the waitress involved in this confrontation effectively ran the store with the help of a co-waitress. The

pair's control of the restaurant was so strong—and self-serving—that one Kendelport waitress refused to work there, though it was closer to her home than Kendelport.

> I [a manager] go to make the shake. She comes over and she says, "The machine is broke." I says, "No, it's not broke." The machine's going on [makes sound of machine]. . . . She says, "No. It's not working." So I'm making a shake and she goes, "That F-ing machine—that God damn F-ing,"—and just took off. . . . I go back to pull the shake [take it off the blender] and she starts [swearing] again. I said, "If you cannot restrain from that language, get off the floor and get off now." She got that [order] book and [makes whizzing sound] she threw it . . . at me. I ducked. I go take care of [her] tables and everything. . . . About an hour and a half later everything calmed down, [and] I happened to see her sitting in the break room. I says, "What are you doing here?" She said, "I'm scheduled till four and I'm not leaving until four." And I says, "You get out of here now." She jumps up and she goes, "I'll cut up every one of them God damn F-ing customer's tires and bust their"—I says, "Lady! You better leave now." And I says, "I'm calling the cops."

The waitress had long ago pronounced the shake machine broken to avoid making milk shakes. She had also proclaimed all dessert ingredients out of stock to avoid making desserts. By insisting on making a shake, the manager, who was working at the store on temporary assignment, challenged the waitress's fiction, threatened her control, and incurred her anger.

Rationalization of Service

As increased productivity was the "rallying cry" of the sixties and marketing the cry of the seventies (Barron 1989), so service has become the battleground of competition of the eighties (Albrecht and Zemke 1985; Phillips et al. 1990). The heightened concern with service is reflected in the explosion of publications expounding the hows and whys of good service, in the proliferation of training programs and seminars designed to raise the service consciousness of managers and employees, and in the appearance of "a new breed of consultant," the service specialist (Barron 1989). The near-religious fervor of the service movement is expressed in the spiritual metaphors that pervade the service literature. Managers are encouraged to take on "the task of evangelism," and "[spread] the word," in order to help frontline workers "maintain an 'otherworldly' focus," and see "the new vision" of service (Albrecht and Zemke 1985); edicts to service workers take the form of commandments—"love thy customer and know thy fish" (McGill 1989)—and are referred to as such (Jerome n.d.; McGill 1989); and service policies are touted as "gospel" (Albrecht and Zemke 1985; Stevenson 1989).

The growing focus on service has stimulated increased efforts to rationalize, and so enhance the quality of service delivery. In accordance with the principles of scientific management, rationalization commences with the separation of conception and execution and culminates in the segmentation and routinization of the work process (Braverman 1974). Arlie Hochschild describes the process and its consequences as applied to the work of flight attendants:

> At Delta Airlines . . . twenty-four men work as "method analysts" in the Standard Practices Divi-

sion of the company. Their job is to update the forty-three manuals that codify work procedure for a series of public-contact jobs. (1983:119–20)

As a result of increasing specialization and standardization in the airlines,

> the overall definition of the task is more rigid than it once was, and the worker's field of choice about what to do is greatly narrowed. Within the boundaries of the job, more and more actual subtasks are specified. Did the flight attendant hand out magazines? How many times? . . . With a smile? (1983:119–20)

In the food service industry, too, service specialists now regulate the work process of frontline employees. SPECs are the culmination of the attempt to rationalize at Route. The thriving Red Lobster chain conducts surveys and interviews to determine its customers' wants and then conveys these to employees in intensive training programs and monthly seminars where, among other things, servers are taught "precisely the phrases to be used" when taking orders (McGill 1989).[8] Prior to certifying dining-room servers, managers at another restaurant chain must verify that a candidate

> greets guest with pleasant, appropriate phrase, giving a choice of seating; makes smiling eye contact with all guests; . . . acknowledges table within two minutes; . . . gives name when taking order; repeats items as guest orders; [engages in] suggestive selling of blackboard specials, cocktails, appetizers, side orders, large beverages, after dinner drinks; when serving food says, "Enjoy your meal. I'll be back to check on

you"; checks back to guest within three minutes; . . . thanks and invites guest to return. (cer-
tification evaluation form, Andy's Restaurant)

In rationalizing the work process, service specialists seek to achieve unprecedented levels of efficiency
and precision in the delivery of service.[9] In the words of
one service magnate: "We believe there is a science to
running dinnerhouse restaurants, . . . a science to determining consumer needs, and a science to answering
those needs, in a disciplined manner, on a massive scale"
(McGill 1989). In the past, service systems have been
"intellectually abandoned and allowed to 'evolve' on their
own" (Albrecht and Zemke 1985:83). Today the delivery
of service is dictated by "service blueprints" produced
by departments of "service engineering" (Albrecht and
Zemke 1985:86; Shostack 1985).

In real estate, the three components of successful
investing have always been *location,* location, location. In service-encounter management, the
components for success might be stated as *details,* details, details. . . . This is management's
responsibility and obligation; a responsibility
that cannot be delegated. With rational, thorough planning, service encounters can be everything management wishes them to be. (Shostack
1985:253)

Because the image the service worker projects
influences the consumer's perception of the company and
of the quality of service received, efforts have also been
made to regulate the server's appearance.[10] Barry Blackman suggests that

---

putting each service technician into a uniform helps create an image or "package" of sameness common to other technicians within the company. This common package fosters a brand image to help assure a purchaser the service will be essentially similar each time he uses it. (1985:300)

Uniforms may even improve the performance of service "technicians."

The uniform actually helps extend management influence to actions of its service technicians; the uniform is an ever-present reminder of management. When a service technician puts on his uniform, he is subordinating part of himself (his freedom to choose his own dress) to company control. (Blackman 1985:301)[11]

Interestingly, many of the dress regulations for waitresses are proscriptive rather than prescriptive, indicating that restaurateurs are concerned with suppressing inappropriate images, as well as projecting desired images. The dress code for Andy's Restaurant proclaims that skirts of uniforms "will be no shorter than 1 and 1/2 inches above the top of the knee cap"; requests that waitresses "avoid elaborate makeup"; and prohibits dark hose, runs, dark-red or brown nail polish, visible hair roots, and "visible tatoos." These injunctions seem intended to ensure that waitresses will not appear cheap, an important consideration in a line of work that has traditionally been identified with promiscuity (Donovan 1920:227–28) and even prostitution. Fifty years ago a girl who left her hometown to become a waitress in the regional metropolis was "generally assumed to have become a prostitute also" (West 1945:28), and there is evidence that for some categories of waitresses the stigma persists. A cocktail waitress interviewed by Spradley and Mann (1975:20), for example, was initially hesitant about serving cocktails because she had always associated bars with "loose living," and thought of "hardcore" barmaids as "hustlers."

The drive to rationalize the appearance and job tasks of the worker and make a "science" out of service has met with limited success at Route. Though the company continues to dissect and refine service procedures on paper, on the floor the waitress continues to regulate the pace and control many of the decisions of her work. She does not execute her job tasks "unthinkingly and without comprehension," but conducts her work in keeping with her own needs and views of efficiency. Ironically, the company's failure to control the work process of front-line employees is partly a function of its success in regulating the work process of those higher up. In divesting managers of decision-making power, depriving them of the power of positive and negative sanctioning, and reducing them to fill-in men, the company helps invest employees with de facto control over their work lives.

From these observations, it can be concluded that the waitress does in fact have something to lose by advancing to the managerial ranks. Insofar as the disempowerment of management is accompanied by the empowerment of frontline workers, movement "up" will entail a loss of freedom and control. For women who would rather walk off the job than submit to interference in their work, this prospective abdication of autonomy may counterbalance the potential benefits of promotion. We shall find, when we return to this issue in the next chapter, that autonomy is not all the waitress stands to lose by ascending the occupational ladder, but it is undoubtedly an important consideration.

5

Up a Crooked Ladder

Congratulations! You walk out of your boss's office. Your palms are sweaty, you feel cold, you're flushed, your head is pounding, your mouth is dry, your stomach feels queasy, your head is spinning, you're excited, happy, and scared out of your wits. What happened?

You've just been promoted!

You're going to be a boss! Who? Yes, you!

—*Natasha Josefowitz*, You're the Boss!

[A manager] asked me, "Would you be interested in going in[to] management?" I just laughed. . . . I just laughed.

—*Route waitress*

Research on white-collar workers in corporate settings reveals that career success is often closely associated with vertical mobility within the organization. In the large, hierarchical corporation studied by Rosabeth Kanter (1977), jobs were evaluated almost entirely on the basis of their potential for advancement. Higher-grade jobs with better pay were turned down if they were known to be dead ends, while sales jobs were sought after because they led into managerial positions. The "be promoted or perish" ethos of the organization was supported by a reward structure in which the intrinsic benefits of work (autonomy, growth, challenge), and most extrinsic benefits (pay, location and furnishings of office), were predicated on advancement. Seniority and increased expertise in one's current position received little formal recognition unless accompanied by a change in title.

In other contexts, it is less clear whether advancement is desired or necessarily desirable. In Chapter 3, evidence was presented that first-line supervisors in industry and in the restaurant have been marginalized from the decision-making process and divested of the power to enforce policy handed down from above. In the restaurant, downgrading of the managerial function compromises the manager's commitment to his work role, contributes to friction between managers and employees, and conduces to high levels of turnover in the managerial ranks. This chapter examines how downgrading of first-line management influences the way in which employees evaluate management as a prospective career.

Definitions of Mobility

Labor mobility can be defined as (1) the ability to change jobs, or move into or out of the work force; (2) the willingness to pursue such moves when opportunities arise; or (3) actual movement between jobs, or into or out of employment (Parnes 1954:13). In addition, two categories of mobility can be distinguished: vertical mobility, which involves a change in social rank, and horizontal mobility, which involves a change in function or occupation (Caplow 1954:59).[1] These subtypes are not mutually exclusive: horizontal mobility frequently involves some alteration of rank, and vertical mobility often entails a change in job function (Caplow 1954:61). This discussion addresses the ability and the propensity of waitresses to move between jobs, as well as actual movement. Both vertical and horizontal mobility are considered.

Hierarchical Structure of the Restaurant

Like the glass and steel skyscraper in which it was housed, the occupational hierarchy of the corporation studied by Kanter (1977) was tall, narrow, and structurally complex. The occupational hierarchy of Route is also like the architectural structure in which it is located: flat and simple. There are four main categories of wage workers in the restaurant: dishwashers, hostesses, cooks, and waitresses. These categories can be ranked from low to high in the order given, with cook and waitress at roughly the same level. Rank refers here to the pay, prestige, and power (ability to enforce one's will) associated with the job. There is, however, considerable variation in the rank of workers within each job category, and it is possible for a full-time, senior dishwasher to wield more power, enjoy higher prestige, and earn more than a part-time, rookie hostess, cook, or waitress.

Whether cooks and waitresses are accurately described as equal in rank is debatable. In general, waitresses earn more than cooks, but an experienced cook makes more than a waitress of similar standing on slow shifts, because his wages are fixed and guaranteed, while hers are contingent upon the restaurant's volume of business. Restaurant cooks score slightly above waiters/waitresses on some occupational prestige scales, but the difference, if any, in prestige enjoyed by cooks and waitresses at Route is small.[2] Relative power is still more difficult to assess. To some extent, waitresses are dependent upon cooks for their financial well-being. A sharp word or impatient request directed at the cook calling the wheel could backfire in half-cooked burgers, mysteriously delayed reorders, and appetizers that appear after the entree. As one waiter explained, "[You] can't go up to the cook and say, 'The food sucks,' because then the rest of your food's going to suck." The following incident illustrates the kind of problems that can arise when cook and waitress are on bad terms.

> About a month and a half ago, I had an order for a grilled chicken dinner and it looked *different,* you know? And I just asked [the cook] very nicely, I go, "Kevy,"—this is something you're *not* supposed to do—I asked Kevy, "Are you sure that this is done?" You know, I didn't want to take it out [deliver it] raw. . . . He goes, "Is it *done?*" And he took the plate away from me and he cut it in half and he showed it to me. He goes, "Does it *look* like it's done to you?" And then he put it back on the plate and *threw* the plate at me and told me, "Now *take* it out." And I said, "Kevy, why did you do that? I am *not* serving this." . . . I went back there [on the line], you know, I was there like, "Fuck you, Kevy!" This was before I went to [the manager].

One waitress who was also a cook said that when she was on the line, orders for a particular waitress tended to turn out "greasy" and "slimy." When asked why, she replied, "Cause I don't like her. That's my revenge."

On the other hand, cooks are more constrained than servers in their relations with management. Like waitresses, cooks are prone to storm off the job in anger, but in their daily interaction with managers they exhibit greater deference and more reserve than workers on the floor. This is probably a reflection of the cook's financial dependence upon the company, which provides the entirety of his income and has the power to award him regular and significant raises. A diligent, punctual, and deferential waitress can hope to make a few cents more in hourly wages than her less exemplary co-servers; but a cook who earns the approval and respect of his employer may earn nearly double the wage of less skilled or favored cooks. Dishwashers too are financially dependent upon the company but rarely remain at the restaurant long enough to cultivate poor or favorable relations with management. There is, in addition, frequently a language barrier between dishwashers who are not native English speakers and managers, making it difficult to evaluate the tenor of their interaction.

Cooks might be considered more valuable than waitresses because they are harder to train, and because an incompetent cook affects more customers than an incompetent waitress. Some waitresses expressed the belief that when a cook and waitress have a falling-out, the waitress is fired because the cook is worth more.

> I basically got fired . . . because of . . . my baby's father. It came down to getting rid of a head cook or me. . . . So [the manager] decided to get rid of me. Cause you'd always get rid of a waitress before you'd get rid of a cook. If you've got a good cook, that can run the line well. Because that's harder to find than a waitress. You can put anybody on the floor and get away with it. Cause there's other people. But in the kitchen you can't.

Another waitress commented:

> Some of the food you even serve is disgusting . . . and you have no choice but to serve it, unless you want to get into a fight with Bennett [a cook]. . . . So you have to basically go along with the system. . . . You can't go to [the manager] and say, "Well, listen. Bennett's giving me these really lousy orders," cause . . . who's he going to fire first? You or Bennett? You [a waitress]. Because it's harder for him to get a cook. . . . I mean, if a cook assaulted a waitress, the cook should have been dismissed. Instead, Tess was fired. I grant you, she probably shouldn't have mouthed off at him, but still.

In the incident referred to here, the leading swing cook and a low-ranking, part-time waitress, who had been arguing through the cooks' window for weeks, became engaged in a physical confrontation that ended with the cook's attempting to submerge the waitress's head in the kitchen sink, the arrival of the police, and threats by the waitress's father to sue the restaurant. The waitress quit Route shortly afterward, having secured another waitressing position prior to the episode, for reasons unrelated to the cook. Though she was not actually fired, this interpretation of her departure demonstrates that some employees believe cooks are more highly valued than waitresses.

In fact, the relative standing of a cook and waitress depends on the status of the individuals involved, not their membership in a particular job category. It is unlikely that anyone would expect Nera, or another high-ranking waitress, to be fired on behalf of a cook, regardless of the cook's status. As a rule, cooks and waitresses interact as equals, and when confrontations occur they occur between workers of comparable standing. Waitresses are as likely to upbraid cooks for their incompetence as cooks are to return the favor. And, though cooks have the power to undermine the waitresses' service, they rarely use it. High-ranking cooks and waitresses, in particular, demonstrate remarkable consideration for one another under acutely stressful conditions. As workers who recognize the complexity and strenuousness of the job each performs, cook and waitress grant one another the appreciation both deserve but rarely receive from a public that accords their work minimal respect.

There are two levels of management in the restaurant: general manager and manager. General managers are paid more and receive bigger bonuses than managers, but there is little perceptible difference in the power or authority of managers of different ranks. The general manager does not issue orders to, or reprimand managers, and managers exhibit no concern for the approval or opinions of the general manager, or of one another. The impression of equality among managers is enhanced by their titles which, unlike the more common labels *assistant manager* and *manager,* do not convey a clear sense of hierarchy. Managers also work different shifts rather than alongside and under the direction of the general manager, so each manager is on his own and in full charge of the restaurant at a given time.

Beyond the individual restaurant there is a district manager, who supervises five or six Route units; and above the district manager is a regional manager who, with two assistants, oversees approximately twelve districts. Employees do not discuss positions in the company above the level of regional manager. The head honchos are known to reside in the central office in California, but there appears to be a conceptual gap between this pinnacle of the organization and the level of regional management.

Horizontal Mobility

Because cook and waitress are the only job categories roughly equal in rank, movement between these jobs is the only avenue of horizontal mobility in the restaurant. No movement from line to floor occurred during the research period. Cooks periodically remarked on how much money waitresses made but expressed no desire to wait tables and tap into this money themselves. Movement from floor to line is also rare. Waitresses do not have much motivation to learn to cook. Working conditions on the line are the worst in the restaurant: cooks work sandwiched between high-temperature grills, vats of boiling grease, continuously flaming burners, and heat lamps (used to keep orders in the window warm). The line has no windows, no air conditioning, and no fans, as any of these would facilitate the cooling of hot orders. In winter the line is insufferably hot; in summer, a virtual oven. Starting pay is low, though a skilled cook may come to make as much as a waitress, and the money is guaranteed.

Waitresses may be deterred from cooking by antagonism from male co-cooks. Mae, one of the few waitresses with formal training as a cook, believed that the presence of competent women on the line threatened the cooks' masculine image.

> I think Charlie had a problem with it. Because not only am I a female, but I'm a white female, which I think . . . threatens Charlie. That a girl could come in and cook better than him? He's

been a cook for how many years? . . . He's been a slow cook for how many years, too? . . . When women go on the line they get a lot of BS from the guys that are already on the line. Cause it's kind of like a macho thing. . . . Like with Charlie and me. It just gets him mad that I cook better than him.

Managers discourage waitresses who express interest in cooking by emphasizing the low pay and poor working conditions on the line. A waitress who had prepped and cooked for the breakfast bar at Andy's prior to coming to Route recalled:

[I asked the manager] if he would let me [cook]. He said no. . . . Because he said that I was too delicate. I was too delicate and that once you get back there and all that grease and whatnot, that my face would break out, you know, and he said that it wasn't a good idea. That's the reason he gave me. . . . That's another thing too. . . . The starting rate, he would only want to pay me like maybe six dollars an hour. Not worth it.

Suggesting to a waitress that she is too delicate to cook may strengthen, rather than diminish, her enthusiasm to learn. One waitress began cooking in direct response to a manager's comment that she would not be able to "take it" on the line.

Waitresses can learn to cook without formal training. Some knowledge of cooking is acquired in the course of waitressing, including how to *read codes* (interpret standard waitress abbreviations for orders and preparation instructions), what size plate goes with which order, which potatoes, gravy, and vegetables go with which entrees, and the meaning of cook–cook and cook–waitress terminology (*all day* = altogether, *down* and *working* = cooking, *eight-six* = not available, or as a command, stop selling). Waitresses learn the layout of the line by watching cooks across the pass bar, and by cooking their customers' orders when it is slow and no cooks are available. This is most likely to occur during shift changes, when one group of cooks departs before its relief has arrived.

> The cooks, at three o'clock, they leave, regardless of whether there's anyone there to cover them, so [the waitress] ends up waiting on tables, seating the customers, cashing them out, cooking their food. . . . Sometimes I had to go back and do dishes, so the customers would have something clean to drink out of.

Only two Kendelport waitresses had formal training as cooks. One, a former convict, was in the process of training when research ended. Apparently, management did not feel she was "too delicate" to endure conditions on the line. The other, Mae, received her training at a different unit, where she became the leading day-shift cook. This position is the most prestigious on the line, because day is the busiest and fastest-paced shift, and because breakfast is the most difficult meal to prepare.[3] Even while serving as the leading day cook, Mae continued to wait tables part time.

> I would go in at seven in the morning with my son, put my son in a highchair on the line, all the way back by the sink, cause I didn't want him around the hot stuff. Give him French toast, cook till eight. At eight the manager would come on the line; I'd run him to the babysitter's. Be back

to work by eight-fifteen. I'd cook till eleven. At eleven o'clock I'd run into the bathroom and throw on a waitress uniform and waitress from eleven to three. I told [my manager], "I want a phone booth in the back, because I want to be able to be Super Woman. . . ." I did that for a year.

She also waitressed on the weekend (her "money days"), so she was off the line when it was most stressful and on the floor when it was most profitable. Mae continued to cook part time when she came to Kendelport and was acknowledged to be among the best cooks in the unit. She returned to waitressing full time following the district manager's refusal to approve her raise on the line. At her previous job, she had threatened to stop cooking when the district manager offered her a raise of twenty-five cents.

[The district manager] called me in the office and he had [the raise] all written up, and he says, "Here's a quarter." And I said, "Mr. Castellano. You can take your quarter and stick it up your *ass.*" And I got up to get my stuff. And he was like, "What's wrong?" I said, "I'm doing good? A quarter? What is a quarter going to do? Is that going to feed my son anymore? Is that going to get him a pair of shoes? You figure out a quarter and you tell me how much more money I'd make a week. Five dollars? Big deal! I don't want five dollars. Forget it. I'd as soon waitress. I ain't cooking no more. That's it. You find a day-shift cook. I ain't cooking no more."

Mae's case suggests that cooking is only profitable for a waitress under limited circumstances: if she is allowed to alternate between line and floor, for instance, and is awarded significant raises. This helps explain why waitresses do not pursue jobs on the line, but fails to explain why cooks do not pursue jobs on the floor. It can only be conjectured that they are hesitant to forfeit the "macho" image of the short-order cook to work in a traditionally female occupation on a female-dominated floor—regardless of the potential benefits in autonomy and earnings.

Horizontal Movement beyond the Restaurant

Movement between Route units or to other restaurant companies is relatively common. This type of mobility may be motivated by financial considerations. Rumor gets out that waitresses at another Route, or a new hotel, make sixty dollars in tips on Tuesday night, and if business at Kendelport is slow, or she has recently suffered an unaccountable string of stiffs, a waitress may contemplate relocation. More often, horizontal moves are prompted by dissatisfaction with working conditions: continued shortages of critical menu items, for example, or a consistent lack of support staff. Frequently, discontent arises around interpersonal relations in the restaurant: a falling-out with a cook and former lover, disapproval of lazy managers, discontent with the growing power base of another waitress, indignation over the persistent rudeness of the restaurant's customers.[4]

Because seniority carries no formal benefits at Route, a waitress forfeits little in pay or privileges by transferring to another unit or seeking employment with a different restaurant.[5] She may suffer a reduction in tip income while she gets her bearings in her new job or if she moves to a restaurant that assigns stations on a seniority basis, but the loss is likely to be temporary given the characteristically high turnover rates among waitresses. Moreover, leaving Route, even under unfavorable circumstances, does not preclude returning at a later date. It is not unheard of for an employee to be rehired by the same manager who fired her months or years earlier. The act of firing is thus not only rare, but, in a measure, meaningless.

Vertical Mobility

Though there is some movement from lower- to higher-ranking wage jobs at Route, movement into management is rare.[6] Only one employee, a waiter, entered the management-training program during the research period. He withdrew after several months.

The lack of movement into management does not reflect an absence of opportunity for advancement. There are only three management positions in a restaurant with forty to fifty employees, but rapid turnover creates frequent openings at the managerial level. The general manager reported that fifteen managers had passed through the Kendelport store in seven years, which means the annual turnover rate for managers was about 70 percent. Nor is movement into management blocked by discrimination. Many of the waitresses questioned on the subject reported that they had been asked to go into management, or enter the management-training program, but had declined the opportunity. Given that the managers who made these proposals themselves suffered from the management shortage, it can be assumed that their intentions were sincere. Promotion campaigns initiated at higher levels in the organization were equally unsuccessful in generating interest in managerial careers. At one point, a two-hundred-dollar reward was offered to employees referring a candidate to the management-training program. At Kendelport the reward was never claimed. The consensus among waitresses was that they would not sell their friends so cheap. In fact, the reward only confirmed the employees' conviction that the company was desperate for managers, and so weakened the respect felt for the managerial position and those who filled it. The company had, in addition, held job fairs in an attempt to recruit managers, but this strategy, too, proved ineffective. According to the general manager, the majority of restaurants in the area were trying to recruit managers: "They're coming up with all kinds of programs, lesser hours, more money, but for some reason it's not being successful."

Since the manager's primary job is to fill in for missing workers, the near absence of movement into management cannot be attributed to a deficiency of requisite skills. A waitress planning to become a manager would need to learn to cook, but waitresses learn much about cooking in the course of waiting tables. A cook aspiring to go into management would theoretically need to learn to pick up, but in practice few managers have more than rudimentary table-waiting skills. Extensive supervisory skills would not be needed, since managers exercise limited authority over their employees and rarely delegate tasks except to dishwashers and rookies, who receive informal task assignments from waitresses and cooks as well. Some waitresses acquire experience drawing up schedules, taking inventory, processing new employees, directing station shifts, calling in dairy orders, and picking up misdirected orders by assisting managers as a way to pass time when business is slow. A number of waitresses had successfully occupied managerial positions in the past and had thereby directly demonstrated their ability to meet the demands of a managerial career.

The only employee who expressed doubt concerning his ability to fill a management position was a waiter, who had turned down an assistant management job at a gas station before coming to Route.

> I declined [the position] because alls I would be doing was actually pumping gas, because there would be no one else to work there. . . . I'd be working seven days a week and a lot of hours and I just didn't need the hassle . . . the hours and being assistant manager of practically nobody, cause nobody was working there. . . . Plus . . . I don't like telling people what they have to do. I just don't like to do that. I like to be at the same level as everybody else. . . . That's just the way I am.

It is significant that a male should voice the desire to "be at the same level as everybody else," since women, not men, have traditionally been credited with a deficient competitive spirit.[7] The waiter's comments are also noteworthy, because they demonstrate that employees do not regard promotion as inherently desirable. The waiter's concern with the hours and hassle involved in management was shared by waitresses evaluating managerial careers at Route. His belief that promotion to management would not be accompanied by an upgrading of job tasks ("alls I would be doing was actually pumping gas") was echoed in the definition waitresses and other employees attached to managerial responsibility.

Evaluations of Management as a Prospective Career

Asked if they had ever considered, or would consider going into management, employees at the restaurant replied:

I would never go into management. Number one, it wouldn't be worth it to me . . . because the headaches, the aggravation, the money. . . . I really do believe they [managers] go through a lot, because they're responsible for that whole unit.

I was given the opportunity to grow into management . . . and I declined it then and I still would decline it now. . . . You have to be totally responsible for an entire shift. That means your dishwashers, your cooks, your waitresses, your performance as an individual on the floor as a manager. . . . I could maintain those positions very well I feel, but I just don't want to gain that extra headache. . . . I wouldn't want it.

When I first went there I was considering it [going into management], but after I was there a while I seen too much of responsibility.

I told him [a manager who suggested she go into management], "You're crazy. I'm not taking it. . . . You couldn't pay me enough to do it."

[A manager] asked me, "Would you be interested in going in[to] management?" I just laughed. . . . I just laughed.

I had the general manager . . . say something to me about it, and I laughed at him.

Of fifteen employees asked, fourteen said they had rejected or claimed they would reject opportunities to go into management. Of these, six had occupied managerial or semimanagerial positions in the past and had subsequently chosen to return to the level of wage worker.

In explaining their motivation for resisting advancement, employees referred to the long hours, low pay, and increased responsibility that would accompany a promotion to the managerial ranks. The apprehension over long hours is easily understood. Employees estimated that managers work between seven and twenty hours a day, six to seven days a week; longer when, as often happened, the three-manager team was depleted by the resignation or transfer of one member. Their observations coincided with those of managers themselves. The general manager maintained that he worked seventy-two to seventy-six hours a week; one supporting manager claimed to put in between ten and fifteen hours a day; the other reported that he had recently gone thirty-two days without a day off, and that during this time he had worked an average of seventy-four hours a week.

Waitresses too work long hours and frequently forgo days off, but whether and when they choose to work overtime, pull a double shift, or come in on their days off is largely up to them. If a waitress is in particular need of cash, she may agree to stay into the next shift when someone calls out, or when there is an unexpected rush. Management is always grateful for volunteers and does not worry about paying waitresses overtime, since their wages are so low. Some waitresses use the restaurant as a kind of emergency cash fund, working there only when their financial situation demands.

> I work there every once in a blue moon. When I feel like I want to work, "Yo. I be right in, okay? Could you put me down for Saturday? I need some money. . . . You need anybody to work graveyard, from one to two o'clock?"

Another waitress commented:

> This week I had to go to work . . . cause I had a telephone bill, electric bill, AT and T phone service come in, so I had to come to work this weekend. But let next weekend roll around, and I get paid too from the state, let me get one pain or a headache, . . . I pick up the phone and say, "Hollinger, my blood pressure up today. I won't be in."

Both these waitresses, and many of their co-waitresses, hold jobs outside the restaurant and have exhausting, but partially flexible, work schedules. It seems probable, therefore, that the waitress's apprehension over the hours involved in management is at root a concern with the lack of control managers have over when and how long they work, and not with the length of their work day.

The concern expressed by employees over the financial consequences of promotion is easily appreciated as well. Though definite knowledge of how incomes compare is rare, it is widely believed that waitresses and cooks earn more than their employers. When hourly as opposed to annual income is compared, even a slow waitress or low-ranking cook can come out ahead as a manager's fixed salary must be spread across sixty- to eighty-hour weeks.[8] The comments of the accountant who moonlighted as a part-time manager at the restaurant provide evidence that these views are more than defensive rationalizations.

> If they ask an employee to go into management, in most cases, especially if the person is a waitress or a waiter or a cook, they're actually going to end up taking a pay cut. . . . I don't think you should

ask an employee to take a pay cut. . . . That's why
they [managers] have . . . a lot of problems.

The speaker's authority on the subject of managerial
versus employee income derives from his many years of
experience helping managers, waitresses, dishwashers,
and cooks at the restaurant complete their income tax
returns.

The concern with responsibility, a recurrent
theme in discussions of promotion, has been discussed at
length in Chapter 3. Here it need only be repeated that
responsibility is defined in negative terms: as a liability
rather than a privilege; as a burden, not a challenge.
Waitresses are also aware that as fill-in man the manager
is at the mercy of his employees, who may call out during
his shift in retaliation for some previous want of consideration on his part. One waitress and waiter, now married
with a baby, consistently called out on a manager they
disliked, causing the manager much apprehension whenever he was scheduled for the couple's shift. Waitresses
who serve as *SCs* and *PICs* are similarly vulnerable to
call-outs from antagonistic co-workers. As one waitress
put it, co-workers are inclined to think, "Yea, I'll call out
on her tonight. I don't like her." The terminology of the
restaurant, in which an employee is said to call out *on* a
manager, reflects the understanding that managers suffer
personally from absenteeism, and that calling out is
therefore something that is done *to* a manager.

The experience of being called out on, and the
sense of vulnerability the experience brings, can discourage waitresses from accepting future offers to SC or
PIC. One waitress recalled the following, not uncommon
episode:

> One night . . . I was service coordinator. Every-
> body went off the floor at eleven o'clock. I had no

cooks, no waitresses, no dishwashers, no nothing. So I had to close the restaurant till I got [someone] coming in. . . . Kaddie [a waitress] didn't show up till almost one o'clock, and somebody else had called out on me, so *I* had to stay on the floor till four-thirty in the morning, cause I had to pick up [wait tables]. . . . It's not hard at all, . . . but I don't think I'd do it again.

Being left with no cooks, waitresses, or dishwashers gives SCs and PICs a taste of the problems involved in management. By asking the more dependable, competent waitresses to SC and PIC, managers may inadvertently deter the most promising candidates from pursuing managerial careers.

Though waitresses did not address the issue explicitly, the forfeiture of autonomy, which would accompany the transition from tipped to salaried employee, must be counted as an additional deterrent to advancement. In contrast to waitresses, managers are directly dependent on the company for their financial well-being and job security. Managers, like wage workers, are in high demand and are not dismissed without strong provocation. Nevertheless, transgressions of organizational policy or failure to meet company standards may bring on a transfer to a potentially less agreeable location. Waitresses are aware that managers, even at relatively advanced levels, are subject to this kind of manipulation by higher-order administrators.

Castellano, he was our district manager for a while, like maybe four years or something. Now Garrison's been our district manager for two years. . . . So they just change the district managers around. Because they feel if one district manager's not doing the right thing and the sales are going down and . . . he's not getting through to any of the managers, then they'll start switching the district managers again. They'll be like, "Oh, Garrison, . . . you're, you're strong. And you can handle Kendelport." Whereas Castellano, he couldn't, so they had to take him down South. They don't leave the company. They just switch them around.

Waitresses are aware too that managers are subject to the humiliation of demotion. One manager at Kendelport had reportedly been the general manager of a different unit and been demoted.[9] Some contend that he got in trouble for making passes at waitresses. Others claim he could not handle the pressure of being general manager. A cook at Kendelport had once been the general manager there but had lost his position after being incarcerated (for reasons unconnected with work), and the district manager was demoted to general manager shortly after research ended.[10] Apart from the monetary losses that accompany a reduction in managerial rank, demoted managers must contend with the discomfort of working alongside, even under, those they once supervised.

It is perhaps because his financial and job security are directly controlled by the company that the manager is more attentive to company directives than are many of his employees. Though a manager is often required to exchange his suit jacket for the dishwasher's vinyl apron, he continues to arrive at work in the appropriate managerial attire. He is willing to work thirty-two days without a break and put in seventy-six-hour weeks, and unlike waitresses, he exhibits reverence and suppresses disdain for his employers (for example, district managers). The manager also exercises greater restraint in his dealings

with the public, tolerating levels of abuse from disgruntled customers that a waitress would find insuffer-
able. In the words of one manager:

> The public, you might say, you end up kissing
> their ass [more] than anything else. . . . You ac-
> cept things that you wouldn't normally accept.
> You go backward to try to be nice, and you still
> don't please them. You try to give them a bit of a
> smile, but sometimes that doesn't work. [To] sum
> it all up, you end up basically kissing their asses.
> That's what it boils down to.

A waitress who returns fire on an angry customer jeopar-
dizes the dollar or two she might have made if she had
suppressed her anger, and runs the risk of the customer
summoning the manager or writing to the district manager. Her potential losses are not great in either case and
are counterbalanced by the satisfaction of venting her
anger, as suggested in the following remarks:

> Cause you depend on them, you got to be nice to
> these suckers. But then sometimes, you forget
> about that niceness and that dollar or two and say,
> in your actions alone, "Kiss my ass, and keep your
> two bucks."

The same waitress recalled her reaction to a customer's
threat to write the district manager as follows:

> I said to myself, "Sucker, write on. You want to
> write? Write. I don't care."

For managers, whose rank and salary ultimately hang in
the balance, it is more difficult to adopt a "kiss my ass" or
"I don't care" attitude toward threatening customers.

The pressure to "accept things that you wouldn't normally accept" is bound to be strong when failure to do "the right thing" might result in transfer or demotion.

Accustomed to defining for herself what the right thing is, the waitress may hesitate to submit to increased constraints on her behavior toward customers and employers. She may also hesitate to place herself in a position in which she is at the mercy of workers who can call out on her, and in which she must regulate her work activities to conform to the needs of employees. The fact that she would not earn significantly more, and might actually make less, for shouldering the burdens of management detracts from the desirability of advancement, as does the low prestige of the managerial role. Several factors that diminish the prestige of management have already been considered, including the association of management with menial duties, such as dishwashing, and the tendency for managers to be newcomers. The management shortage helps compromise respect for the managerial role and for those who fill it, as management comes to be seen as a job nobody wants, and anyone can have.

> They [Route] just don't have the help. Nobody wants to put in applications [to be] managers, and they just don't have the help. And it's a shame, but we're stuck with Mr. Hollinger. We're stuck with Innes. And this new guy that just came in, . . . he was a service assistant [dishwasher]. He doesn't know *anything* about cooking. I mean, they're getting these people off the street practically to come in here.

The shortage of managers is believed to affect the quality of management at higher levels in the organization as well.

> All those managers are crooked. The district
> managers are crooked. . . . One district manager
> was a cop. Got fired from the police force, be-
> cause he took evidence, you know, stuff when
> they confiscate? Jewels? He's got a big diamond
> ring, this big on his finger. Another district man-
> ager got fired from [another restaurant chain] for
> tapping into funds. Was at Route for a *long* time.

Asked why the company hired "crooked" managers, the
waitress quoted here responded, "Because Route is desperate right now. . . . I just think it's desperation." A
cycle thus emerges in which low prestige conduces to the
management shortage, which in turn further undercuts
respect for the managerial role.

Implications for the Status of Women
in the Work Force

The growing number of women in entry-level
managerial positions has been claimed as a partial success
by those concerned with the status of women in the work
force. There is still concern that women in these positions earn less than their male counterparts, possess less
authority, and have fewer opportunities to advance beyond the lower and middle levels of management (Moore
1986:1; Powell 1988:13). The evidence from Route suggests that in some cases, the arrival of women in entry-
level positions would be less than a partial success; it
would be a failure, signaling the downgrading of management, rather than the upgrading of women's status. First-
line managerial positions at Route have few intrinsic or
extrinsic benefits to offer their incumbents. Managers are
excluded from the decision-making process and exercise

little authority over wage workers. Their responsibilities, which consist largely in filling in for absent dishwashers and cooks, diminish rather than enhance the prestige of their position and render them vulnerable to unreliable, unpredictable, and occasionally vindictive employees. Managers work long hours and are often compelled to forgo days off, and because they are not compensated for overtime, they suffer the final insult of making less on an hourly and perhaps an annual basis than those they supervise.

The "failure" of the waitress to pursue a managerial career in the restaurant testifies to her ability to evaluate the structure of rewards critically: to look beyond a promising title to a reality of petty tasks. Typically interpreted as a sign of female passivity or powerlessness, the absence of upward mobility in this case reflects the worker's determined refusal to exchange the benefits of her current position for the false promises of promotion. Moreover, while the waitress rejects the possibility of success through advancement, she strives to improve her position at work through alternative methods: by engaging in horizontal mobility, by directing the flow of customers through the restaurant, and by exploiting the manager's role as fill-in man to assert and defend her autonomy. Only when the definition of action is restricted to upward movement can the waitress be defined as passive. Only when upward mobility is blindly equated with success can the waitress who rejects advancement be said to fail.

6

Resisting the Symbolism of Service

In the public world of work, it is often part of an individual's job to accept uneven exchanges, to be treated with disrespect or anger by a client, all the while closeting into fantasy the anger one would like to respond with. Where the customer is king, unequal exchanges are normal, and from the beginning customer and client assume different rights to feeling and display.

—*Arlie Hochschild*, The Managed Heart

[The customer] jumps up, he pushes me out of the way, and he goes, "You just blew your tip! I'm going to have your *job!* That's what I'm going to have." . . . I don't take that. . . . I have to tell people off. When they're degrading me personally, then I will tell them, "I don't have to put up with your shit. I don't have to wait on you. I don't have to. You can leave."

—*Route waitress*

Employees of service industries are encouraged to treat customers with unflinching reverence and solicitude; to regard their concerns and needs as paramount; to look upon them as masters and kings. But to accept this

---

131

image of the other requires that one adopt a particular image of self. If the customer is king (or queen), the employee by extension is subject, or servant. In the restaurant, a complex system of symbolism encourages customer and worker alike to approach service as an encounter between beings of vastly different social standing, with unequal claims to courtesy, consideration, and respect. Though the customer accepts the imagery of servitude and adopts an interactive posture appropriate to the role of master, the waitress rejects the role of servant in favor of images of self in which she is an active and controlling force in the service encounter. Perhaps because of this, she is able to control the feelings she experiences and expresses toward her customers, and she is neither disoriented nor self-alienated by the emotional demands of her work.

Waitress as Servant: Company- and Customer-backed Metaphors

Conventions of Interaction

The image of waitress as servant is fostered above all by the conventions that govern interaction between server and served. Much as domestic servants in the nineteenth century did not dine with or in the presence of masters, so today waitresses are forbidden to take breaks, sit, smoke, eat, or drink in the presence of customers.[1] At Route, employees are not allowed to consume so much as a glass of water on the floor, though they are welcome to imbibe unlimited quantities of soda and coffee out of sight of customers. The prohibition against engaging in such physically necessary acts as eating, drinking, and resting in the customer's presence functions to limit contact between server and served and fortify status lines. It is, in addition, a means of concealing the humanness of those whom one would like to deny the courtesies of personhood. When indications of the server's personhood inadvertently obtrude into the service encounter, customers may be forced to modify their interactive stance. One Route waitress commented that when her parents ate at the restaurant her customers treated her with greater respect.

> They look at me like, "Oh my God. They have *parents*?" It's sometimes like we're not human. It's like they become more friendly when my parents are there and I get better tips off them. And I've never gotten stiffed when my parents have been sitting there. . . . They see that outside of this place I am a person and I have relationships with other people.

Physical Setting and Costumes of Waitress Work

The architecture of nineteenth-century houses reinforced class distinctions by ensuring physical segregation of master and servant (Sutherland 1981:30). Servants were charged to enter and exit through back doors and were exiled to live and work in isolated and barren quarters.[2] Special care was taken to conceal or separate the kitchen from family living areas. Similarly, in restaurants, employees may be required to enter through back doors or don street clothes, and so assume the status of customer, if entering through the front door. They are assigned separate bathrooms and separate rooms to eat and rest in, and the kitchen is carefully camouflaged behind swinging doors or staggered partitions. Even then, proximity to the kitchen diminishes the desirability of a table, indicating that the polluting force of servants cannot be contained by physical barriers.

The demarcation between the quarters of server and served is marked in the restaurant, as in a house, by a change in decor: the carpet stops abruptly at the boundary between front and back house; the soft lighting of the dining room is replaced by a fluorescent glare; and no music is piped into the employees' working areas, break room, or bathrooms. As one moves into the work areas of lower-ranking employees the decor becomes increasingly barren. Like scullery maids who "never entered family quarters, . . . and ate and slept in nooks and crannies" (Sutherland 1981:30), dishwashers and other back-house employees rarely appear on the floor but are kept out of sight in rooms with no windows, no air conditioning, and drains in the floor. It may be symbolically significant that at Route, as in many restaurants, the managers' office is located in the bowels of the back house, squeezed between the employee bathrooms, the dish room, and the cooks' line.

It has already been suggested that the waitress is discouraged from adorning herself in a way that might appear cheap. She is also discouraged from dressing above her station. The common interdiction in service dress codes against conspicuous jewelry may serve the same purpose as medieval decrees forbidding low-ranking persons to wear gold (Simmel 1950:343). In each case those of subordinate status are prohibited from assuming symbols of wealth or status that might obscure their position and blur class lines. The aggressively plain uniform of the waitress underscores status distinctions between those who render and those who receive service in the same way that the black dress and white cap of the nineteenth-century domestic acted as a "public announcement of subservience" (Rothman 1987:169; Sutherland 1981:29–30). Today the standard uniform of the waitress (plain dress and apron or pinafore) and that of a maid are similar enough that it is difficult to determine whether certain drawings in school textbooks represent waitresses or maids (Federbush 1974:181). In the modern service encounter, the need to underscore the server's inferiority may be especially strong as the status differential between server and served is intrinsically tenuous. The superiority of customer to waitress is limited temporally to the duration of the encounter and spatially to the boundaries of the restaurant. Rigidly defined dress codes, which eliminate all clues of the server's nonwork status, may serve to put the customer at ease in issuing orders to one whose subordination is so narrowly defined.

It is in their implications for the worker's status that the dress codes of direct services differ from those of other categories of work. As the titles suggest, blue- and white-collar workers are also subject to dress codes, but the primary function of these codes is not to proclaim the worker's low social standing or control her projected personality. The appearance regulations of factory workers are designed at least partly with the security of the company and the safety of the worker in mind.[3] The appearance codes of service workers are concerned primarily with image and status delineation and may actually interfere with the worker's ability to perform her job safely or effectively. Some flight attendants are required to wear heels, which decrease their stability and increase their fatigue (Hochschild 1983). And in some restaurants, waitresses who carry plates on their arms rather than on trays are required to wear short-sleeved, and hence less authoritative uniforms.[4] Because plates are heated (by heat lamps or in the oven) to keep the food warm, waitresses

135

must allow the plates (and the food) to cool, or pad their arms with napkins before delivering orders. Both strategies waste time and produce lukewarm food, and the latter can lead to burned arms, as napkins tend to absorb heat or fly away en route to the table.

The businesswoman who would "dress for success" is, like the waitress, subject to dress regulations of remarkable specificity. She is advised by a bestselling dress manual to wear a wool skirt with ample hem, reinforced waist, and zipper the same color as the fabric. She is counseled to wear dark pumps, closed at the heel and toe, with one-and-a-half-inch heels, and she is urged to carry an umbrella with at least ten spokes, preferably solid (Molloy 1977). While the waitress's maidlike uniform functions to diminish her status, however, the executive's "uniform" is designed for status enhancement. A basic dress-for-success guideline is "always wear upper-middle-class clothing" (Molloy 1977:186).[5] The uniform of the executive also differs from that of the service worker in that it is at least ostensibly voluntary, indicating that however strictly the businessperson's appearance is controlled by her work, this control is not recognized as a right.

Linguistic Conventions of Service

The linguistic conventions of the restaurant and, in particular, the unilateral use of first names, further emphasize status differences between customer and waitress. Like the nonreciprocal use of terms of endearment (Wolfson and Manes 1980), the unilateral use of first names signals the subordinate status of the addressee; thus, African Americans, children, and household domestics have traditionally been addressed by first names by those whom they in turn address as *sir, ma'am, Mr.* or

Mrs. Restaurants perpetuate this practice by requiring servers to wear name tags which, regardless of the worker's age, bear only her first name, and by requiring servers to introduce themselves by first name to each party they wait on. Waitresses generally have no access to the customer's first or last name (the customer's larger "information preserve" prohibits inquiry) and are constrained to resort to the polite address forms *sir* and *ma'am* when addressing their parties.[6]

The etymological nearness of the terms *service worker* and *server/servant* to *servile* (Hollander 1985:56) contributes to the imagery of servitude by providing linguistic continuity between historically stigmatized and modern forms of service. Throughout the nineteenth century domestic workers rebelled against the label *servant,* which carried connotations of serfdom, indentured servitude, and slavery. As a result of this rebellion, euphemisms such as *help* were gradually substituted for the implicitly demeaning *servant* (Sutherland 1981:125). The term *server,* a relatively new innovation in the restaurant industry (Jerome n.d.), is thus anachronistic rather than conservative and suggests a desire to resurrect more traditional forms of service.

The symbolism of service is not a creation of Route, or of other service industries in which it is found. The symbolic similarities between direct-service work and domestic servitude are the product of actual historical connections between past and present forms of service. The proliferation of restaurants in the early twentieth century coincided with the appearance of smaller, mechanized houses and the corresponding disappearance of the domestic servant as an essential fixture in middle- and upper-middle-class homes (Sutherland 1981:182–99). It seems likely that the symbolism of service was simply transported along with the physical and social functions of the domestic from private home to private enterprise.

Even so, modern service organizations must be charged with actively perpetuating the conventions of servitude and, in some cases, inventing new conventions that restate ties with the past. The restaurant requires the waitress to dress as a maid and introduce herself by first name; the restaurant commissions the building of separate bathrooms for employee and customer; and the restaurant promotes the degrading term *server*. In preserving the conventions of servitude the company encourages the waitress to internalize an image of self as servant and to adopt an interactive stance consistent with this image. In promoting an image of server as servant to the public, the restaurant encourages customers to treat, or mistreat, the waitress as they would a member of a historically degraded class.

Public Perceptions of Service as Servitude

That customers embrace the service-as-servitude metaphor is evidenced by the way they speak to and about service workers. Virtually every rule of etiquette is violated by customers in their interaction with the waitress: the waitress can be interrupted; she can be addressed with the mouth full; she can be ignored and stared at; and she can be subjected to unrestrained anger. Lacking the status of a person she, like the servant, is refused the most basic considerations of polite interaction. She is, in addition, the subject of chronic criticism. Just as in the nineteenth century servants were perceived as ignorant, slow, lazy, indifferent, and immoral (Sutherland 1981), so in the twentieth century service workers are condemned for their stupidity, apathy, slowness, incompetence, and questionable moral character. The full range of criticism commonly directed toward service workers is captured in a 1987 *Time* cover story entitled "Pul-eeze! Will Somebody Help Me?" (Koepp 1987). The article and its accompanying cartoons portray service workers as ignorant: cabdrivers do not know where Main Street is, and bookstore cashiers have never heard of Dickens; incompetent: a clerk in an appliance store "does not know how to turn on the tape recorder he is trying to sell"; lazy: men at work play cards and smoke, while painters snooze; and immoral: cabin attendants "stand by unconcerned, aloof and bored, while old folks and children struggle with their bags." The *Time* story is not unique. Television commercials regularly caricature the ineptitude of service workers, and newspapers and magazines are inundated with articles bemoaning the service problem, as newspapers and magazines in the last decades of the last century were flooded with articles on the "servant problem" (Sutherland 1981:169–71).[7]

Criticism of service is not confined to television or to the pages of popular journalism. One of the most impassioned denunciations of service workers is found in Marvin Harris's anthropological text, *America Now.* Harris (1981:39–59) describes service workers as hostile, physically and vocally abusive, disinterested, incompetent, arrogant, snarling, evasive, unreliable, unrepentant, bored, apathetic, rude, and threatening. He accuses service workers of crimes commensurate with their moral and mental deficiencies: bus drivers drive recklessly, caterers poison food, filling station attendants assault customers, doctors and nurses send families home with the wrong babies and let patients bleed to death.[8] Harris's commentary confirms that service workers have inherited the negative stereotypes as well as the physical and social functions of their nineteenth-century predecessors, and demonstrates that anthropologists are as much imprisoned by the values and beliefs of their culture as are those they study.

As service workers have inherited the negative stereotypes of servants, so modern consumers have inherited a belief in a "golden age" of service. In the past the date of this golden age was not fixed, but according to Daniel Sutherland (1981:6), seemed to advance with the passing of generations: "By the mid-1870s, the golden age was estimated to be around 1850, . . . In the twentieth century, those halcyon days were remembered as being in the decade after the Civil War, and by 1920, they had progressed as far as 1900." Stephen Koepp (1987) identifies the early post–World War II era as the "heyday of personal service," indicating that the golden age of service continues to advance—or retreat. Still more recently, the ideal of personal service has come to be located, not in the past, but in other countries, most notably Japan (Barron 1989).

The imagery of servitude is the most insidious and perhaps, therefore, the most dangerous of hazards the waitress encounters. It pervades every aspect of her work, pressuring her to internalize a negative perception of self and assume a corresponding posture of submission; yet, because it is symbolically conveyed and not, for the most part, explicitly advocated, it cannot be directly confronted and may not even be consciously recognized. Nevertheless, the Route waitress successfully resists the symbolism of service, counterpoising company-supported understandings of her role as servant with her own images of self as a soldier confronting enemy forces, or alternatively, as an independent businessperson, working in her own interests, on her own territory.

Waitress as Soldier

If asked, a waitress would certainly agree that waiting tables is much like doing battle, but waitresses do not voluntarily make the comparison explicit. Rather, the perception of waiting tables as waging war and accordingly, the self-perception of waitress as soldier, is expressed implicitly in the waitress's war-oriented terminology: groups of tables under the control of individual waitresses are referred to as *stations*; the cooks' work area is referred to as the *line*; simultaneously adding several checks to the cooks' wheel is *sandbagging*; to receive many customers at once is to *get hit*; a full station or busy line is *bombed out*; old food and empty restaurants are *dead*; customers who leave no tips, *stiff*; abbreviations used by the waitress to communicate orders to the cook are *codes*; to get angry at someone is to *go off on* or *blow up at* her; to be short an item of food on an order is to *drag* the item; the number of customers served is a *customer count*; the late shift is *graveyard* or *grave*; to provide assistance to a co-worker (especially a cook) is to *bail him out*. Waitresses occasionally devise new uses of the war idiom. One waitress commented that when she was pregnant she had her friend *run* the eggs while she went to throw up. Later, when her manager refused to let her go home, the waitress responded by handing him her book and walking out: "I walked off my—I abandoned ship," she recalled. Explaining why she objected to a manager having an affair with a waitress, another waitress commented that managers "don't supposed to infiltrate the treaty."

Though much of this is official company terminology, it assumes the connotations of battle only in connection with the waitress's informal, and more blatantly war-oriented language. To refer to the nucleus of the kitchen as the *line* does not in itself convey a sense of combat; there are assembly lines and bus lines as well as lines of fire and battle. Only when the cooks' line is regularly said to be *bombed out*, or when stations are repeatedly referred to as *getting hit*, does the battle-oriented meaning of these terms become apparent.

Several of the war idioms used by waitresses are not specific to restaurant work but are used in other occupations, or are common slang. The point here is not that the waitress's view of her work is unique, but that it is a view very different from that promoted by the physical props and interactive conventions of the restaurant. Like many people, and seemingly to a greater degree, the waitress views her work as something of a battle and those with whom her work brings her into contact as the enemy. More important, she views herself, not as a servant who peacefully surrenders to the commands of her master, but as a soldier actively returning fire on hostile forces. The waitress's capacity to sustain this self-image while donning the costume of a maid and complying with the interpersonal conventions of servitude, attests to her strength of will and power of resistance. The same may be said of all subordinate persons who are forced to resist without openly violating the symbolic order (Scott 1985:33).

Waitress as Private Entrepreneur

During a rush, when the restaurant looks and sounds like a battle zone, the metaphor of service as war and waitress as soldier is most salient. During more peaceful periods, a different image of self assumes prominence: that of waitress as private entrepreneur. While these perceptions of self can be viewed as divergent and even opposed, both convey a sense of power and action.[9]

Evidence that the waitress perceives herself as a private entrepreneur is found in her conceptual isolation of herself from the company and in her possessiveness toward people and things under her jurisdiction. The waitress's self-isolation may be expressed relatively directly, as in the following comments of a Route waitress:

> When she [a dissatisfied customer] was getting ready to pay her check, I was ringing it up and she was asking me my name, she was asking my manager's name, she was writing down the regional office's number. So I said, "Look. Do you have a problem? I'm a grown woman. If you have a problem with me, talk to me. If you have a problem with Route, call the region. Fine. If you have a problem with me, talk to me."

It is also expressed in the waitress's ambivalence toward performing tasks not directly related to the business of making tips. As an independent businessperson, the waitress views her responsibilities to the company as extremely limited. The company pays her a minor retainer, but it is felt to cover few duties beyond those immediately related to waiting tables. Accordingly, *sidework* (stocking supplies and cleaning other than that involved in bussing tables) is performed by the waitress with an air of forbearance as though it were understood that such work was above the call of duty.

The term *sidework* fosters the view that these tasks are peripheral to the waitress's work, but in fact, the thorough completion of sidework duties is critical to the smooth functioning of each shift—and to peaceful relations between shifts. The failure of swing waitresses to

stock chocolate fudge spells disaster for grave waitresses
faced with twenty orders for sundaes and no supplies.
Likewise, the neglect of grave waitresses to fill the syrup
dispensers and stock butter creates chaos for the day
shift. There is rarely time to stock the necessary items
while waiting tables: supplies are often packed in boxes
under other boxes on shelves in locked rooms or freezers;
they are packaged in jumbo cans and jars, which are
heavy and difficult to open; and they sometimes require
heating or defrosting before they can be used. Still, stocking and cleaning for the next shift are peripheral to the
waitress's work in the sense that they do not directly
enhance her tip earnings, and this is the sense that is
most significant for the waitress as entrepreneur.

The waitress may, in addition, consider it beyond
the call of duty to intervene on the company's behalf to
prevent theft of restaurant property.

> I constantly tell Hollinger [a manager] he's a jerk.
> Constantly. Cause he's an ass. Because, people
> came in and ripped off place mats on graveyard,
> and he came in giving me heck. . . . And I said,
> "Let me tell you something, Hollinger. I don't
> *care* if they rip off the place mats. If you want
> somebody to stand by that door, and by that regis-
> ter, then you'd better hire somebody just to do
> that. Cause that's not my job. I'm here to wait on
> the people. I take the cash.[10] I can't be baby-
> sitting grown adults."

The place mats referred to here were being sold by Route
as part of a promotional campaign; waitresses do not use
place mats to set tables. The point is significant because,
as will be seen, waitresses are extremely possessive of,
and so likely to protect, restaurant property that they use
in their work.

The waitress's tendency to isolate herself from the company, which she perceives as neither liable for her faults nor warranted in requiring her to do more than wait tables, indicates that she does not see herself as an employee in the conventional sense. As discussed previously, her sense of independence is fostered by the tipping system, which releases her from financial dependence on the company, and by the circumscription of managerial authority, which indirectly augments the scope of her autonomy. At the same time, the waitress's perception that she is in business for herself may prompt her to assert her independence more strongly.

In keeping with her self-image as entrepreneur, the waitress refers to restaurant property as though it belonged to her. She speaks of *my* salt and peppers, my coffee, my napkins, my silverware, my booths, my catsups, my sugars. Linguistically, people too belong to the waitress who talks of *my* customers, my district manager, and my manager. The inclusion of managers among the waitress's possessions reflects her view of managers as individuals hired by the company to maintain satisfactory working conditions so she can conduct her business efficiently. Cooks, dishwashers, and hostesses, on the other hand, tend to be viewed as employees hired by and accountable to managers and are referred to more inclusively as *our* or *their* (the managers').

The waitress also exhibits possessiveness in the way she treats her belongings and the belongings of others. Though she is unwilling to discourage customers from stealing company place mats, she may protect items she uses, and so regards as her own, literally to the knife:

> [A customer] comes in, and he wanted a to-go order of a steak and so forth and he had a steak knife, and silverware. . . . I watched him take it

[the silverware]. And I told him . . . "I won't give you your food until you give me back *my* silverware." I was determined not to give him his to-go order until he gave me back my silverware, and he was determined he was taking it with the silverware. So he pulled a knife [his own] on me and told me, how would I like my pretty little face all cut up? And not to get smart with him and so forth. So I just yelled for Calvin [a cook] and said, "I'm not getting smart with you. You give me back my silverware, you'll get your food." (emphasis added)

If waitresses are adamantly protective of their own property, they are equally respectful of the property of others. In the restaurant, ownership is determined by location: supplies located in a waitress's station belong to her for the duration of the shift. (Customers who pilfer napkins, silverware, and salt and pepper shakers from nearby tables are often inadvertently stealing from another waitress's station.) A waitress who wishes to borrow a co-waitress's catsups, silverware, napkins, or coffee must ask to do so. If she cannot locate the owner and is in desperate and immediate need of the item, she may take it but will apologetically inform the owner as soon as possible that she "stole" the needed article. Borrowing or stealing customers is never acceptable. Apart from those rare occasions when she has obtained her co-worker's consent beforehand, a waitress will not take the order of a party seated in a co-worker's station no matter how frantically the customers wave menus, or how impatiently they glare at passing employees. If, as frequently happens, the "owner" of the party has disappeared, or if there is some confusion concerning the party's ownership, a waitress will search the corners of the restaurant and question every employee in an effort to locate or identify the rightful owner, rather than take the order herself and risk being accused of theft.[11] Indeed, waitresses avoid becoming involved with their co-workers' customers, even in the interests of lending assistance. One waitress recalled that a co-waitress and friend had been caught in the cross fire of a customer food fight and had been doused with orange soda. Asked if she had intervened on behalf of her friend and reprimanded the customers, the waitress responded, "No. I didn't say nothing. Cause that's Mary's people."

If a waitress does lend assistance to a co-worker's party, she is likely to approach the party's owner immediately afterward and explain what she has done and why (for example, "I gave table six some napkins, cause the kid spilled his water"). This allows the party's owner to keep track of what her customers have and still need and ensures that chargeable items will be added to the check. Equally important, by explaining her presence in a co-worker's domain, the waitress concedes that she has trespassed and acknowledges her co-worker's right to sovereignty on her own territory.

A waitress who is flagged down by a particularly aggressive party in a co-worker's station is liable to lose substantial time from her own parties listening to the customers' questions or complaints, tracking down their rightful waitress, or fulfilling their requests personally. In these instances, the waitress may inform the party's owner of her assistance as a means of pointing out that, by virtue of her negligence, the owner has trespassed on the assisting waitress's time. The negligent waitress typically apologizes (sincerely) and then goes on to criticize the party for its relentless requests or complaints. The assisting waitress agrees that the customers appeared rude or picky, or simply expresses sympathy with her co-worker and so demonstrates that the waitress's negligence is forgiven. These interchanges do not function to establish a balance of debt between servers. A waitress who lends assistance in such cases does not expect and will not ask for a return favor at a later date. These relatively formalized interactions serve only to reaffirm the sanctity of each waitress's time and territory by acknowledging that a violation of the possessive order has taken place.

The emphasis waitresses place on respecting one another's property and territorial boundaries is part of a broader code of noninterference. As entrepreneurs operating on their own and in their own interests, waitresses do not expect to be interfered with by others. The anger that the waitress experiences in response to managerial intervention in her work (discussed in Chapter 4) may arise, in part, because such intervention is at variance with her understanding of her status in the restaurant as an independent businessperson. Waitresses also expect each other to respect their autonomy and rarely meddle with the work habits of co-workers. Some waitresses apparently define good relations with co-workers and management as those involving minimum contact. One former Route waitress commented:

> I got along with all the managers [at Route]. Nobody bothered me.

Another waitress remarked:

> Route right now, it's fun. I don't get any abuse, I don't get any hassles. It's just fun. And I don't really pay attention to anybody.

And another said:

Graveyard staff, they're the easiest to get along with. They mind their own business, and they're not as petty as any of the other staffs.

One of the clearest manifestations of the waitresses' code of noninterference is the diversity of methods they employ to carry food. Some Route waitresses can stack ten or more plates on one arm and carry two in their spare hand; others can barely manage three plates at a time, and still others resort to carrying plates on beverage trays. Some waitresses can hold five full water glasses in one palm or carry two brimming coffee cups on saucers in one hand without spilling a drop; others can manage only three glasses or two cups with both hands and are still prone to slosh and spill their beverages en route to the table. There is a proper, or optimally efficient, method of carrying plates and glasses, and it is fairly easy to learn; yet those who are familiar with the technique do not attempt to teach it to less-skilled workers, and these in turn do not solicit instruction from their more efficient co-waitresses. This is not a case of seasoned workers guarding trade secrets, for some experienced, high-ranking waitresses carry plates relatively inefficiently, and there is no attitude of condescension or mystery among those who possess the skill. It would simply be inconsistent with the waitress's emphasis on protecting her autonomy, and respecting that of others, to correct or even comment on the carrying practices or other work habits of her co-workers.

One of the few instances in which a waitress directly interfered with the work of a co-waitress ended in a physical confrontation. In this incident a longtime Route waitress advised a relative newcomer not to scoop ice from the ice bin with a glass, since the glass might break, and the bin would then have to be emptied and flushed.

The newcomer advised the waitress to mind her own business and continued to use the glass to scoop ice, dragging it along the metal bottom of the bin in the process. The first waitress then called in a manager to back her up, and the two waitresses continued to exchange sharp words while he stood between them. Finally, tempers peaked and the newcomer reached around the manager and slapped her co-worker in the face. There were other issues underlying this conflict, including quite possibly racial tensions, but it is significant that the final confrontation took the form of a dispute over the right of one waitress to intervene in the work of another. In discussing the incident with her co-workers afterward, the senior-ranking waitress took great care to justify her initial interference, pointing out that not only were customers likely to get glass slivers in their soda, but she herself was in danger of suffering injuries since she used ice from that bin for her own drinks.

Freedom of Emotion

As she resists company efforts to influence her perception of self, so the waitress maintains control over the emotions she experiences and, to some degree, expresses in the service encounter. The waitress may adopt a submissive or energetically friendly manner toward those she serves, but she recognizes this manipulation of self as a means of manipulating the other. The boundary between front and backstage, between manufactured and spontaneous emotion, remains distinct; even in the midst of a performance the waitress does not lose herself in her role or lose sight of her objective.

This is my motto: "You sit in my station at Route, I'll sell you the world. I'll tell you anything you

want to hear." Last night I had this guy, wanted
my phone number. He was driving me nuts. And
I wasn't interested. . . . He goes, "Well, how
come you and your husband broke up?" I said,
"Well, he found out about my boyfriend and got
mad. I don't know. I don't understand it myself."
And he started laughing. And I'm thinking, *"This
is my money. I'll tell you anything."* . . . I got five
bucks out of him. He didn't get my phone number, but *I got my five-dollar tip.* I'll sell you the
world if you're in my station. (emphasis added)

The waitress does not sell her customer the world, only a
moment of cheerful banter and an illusion of friendship.
For this sale she is adequately compensated: "I got my
five-dollar tip"—as though she had settled beforehand on
a fair price for her illusion.

The success of such an encounter is not measured
by monetary rewards alone, however. For the waitress as
for all social actors, skillful dissimulation may be an exercise in autonomy, an expression of control.

By easily showing a regard that he does not have,
the actor can feel that he is preserving a kind of
inner autonomy, holding off the ceremonial order
by the very act of upholding it. And of course in
scrupulously observing the proper forms he may
find that he is free to insinuate all kinds of disregard by carefully modifying intonation, pronunci-
ation, pacing, and so forth. (Goffman 1967:58)

The degree of control the waitress maintains over her
inner state is suggested by the ease with which she turns
on and off the facade of subservience or conviviality: a
smile becomes a sneer even as she turns away from the
table; "yes, ma'am, yes, sir" become vehement expletives as soon as she disappears behind the lines.

I can cuss like a wizard now. Because when they
get on your nerves you go in the back and before
you know it you saying, "You motherfucker, you
God damn bastard, you blue-eyed faggot." . . . I
came out with some names I ain't never thought I
knew.

Many servers commented that waitressing had
made them tougher and had, in addition, altered their
perception of the public.

It's changed me a lot. I have less patience with
the public. I found out how rude and cruel people
today are. . . . I seen two faces of the public, and
I don't like it. I don't like their evil side. . . .
After you been working with the public for X
amount of years, you start seeing the good and
the bad in people, and the bad outweighs the
good.

My thoughts on people went downhill after being
on graveyard for a while. . . . I was never hit with
ignorance or someone speaking to me gruffly or
roughly and ordering around, and snapping their
fingers. . . . People basically are not nice people.

I never knew that people were so low-down, rot-
ten, and whatever that goes along with it until
you start waitressing. . . . I never knew in my life
how rude and nasty and obnoxious people can be.
Until you start waitressing and you have to wait
on these people. . . . [later] They act like ani-
mals! Like, like they starving. Like they ain't
never had a piece of gristle or toast in their
mouth!

As the waitress comes to see the public in an increasingly negative light, she comes to interpret her customers' rudeness and impatience, like their low tips, as evidence of their "evil side," and not a reflection on her waitressing or social skills. In turn, she becomes less willing to tolerate impatience and irritation which she no longer accepts responsibility for provoking. In the terms of her own idiom of war, the waitress claims the right to return fire on what she has come to regard as inherently aggressive, hostile forces.

> The worst experience I had as far as a customer was when I worked graveyard and a family came in . . . two girls and a man and a woman. She obviously was a foreigner, cause she spoke broken English. . . . And she was very rude, very nasty to me. . . . First thing that she did when she sat down was complain. From the time she sat down to the time they ended up walking out, she complained left and right. And she embarrassed me. She tried to embarrass me. She tried everything in the book. She degraded me. But I stood up to her, and I wouldn't let that happen. I stood up to her regardless of whether they were customers, regardless of whether I lost my job.[12] Nobody's going to degrade me like that because I'm a waitress. . . . And then she started getting loud. And boisterous. . . . I said, "Look." And then I put my book down. I slammed my book down. I put my pen on the table. . . . I said, "Look. If you can do a better job than me, then you write your damn order down yourself and I'll bring it back to the kitchen. When it's ready I'll let you know, and you go back there and pick it up." *Then* she called me a foreigner. And that's

when the shit hit the fan. I said, "How dare you have the gall to call me a foreigner? *You're* the one that's in America. *You're* the foreigner. The problem with you foreigners, is *you* come in this country and *you* try and boot Americans out of their *own* jobs, their *own* homes, and you try and take over this country." I said, "Don't you *ever* call me a foreigner, lady. Because I'll take you right by your collar now. I don't care whether I lose my job or not." *Then* she started cursing at me, and then I cursed right back at her. . . . Then she started arguing with her husband. . . . Called him a MF, bad, bad, vulgar language, right? . . . And he said, "If you call me that one more time . . . I'm going to knock you right in your MFing mouth. And I'll put you on the ground in front of everybody." And she deserved it, and when he said it, I applauded him. I said, "Boy, I'll tell you. If I was married to a bitch like her, I would have knocked her out a long time ago." And he just smiled at me and turned around and walked out.

The waitress slams down her book immediately before releasing her anger on the woman, thereby signaling that she is no longer willing to play the role of compliant servant: she is going to take a stand as a person. In breaking character and expressing her anger she defies company- and customer-supported conceptions of the waitress as one obligated to endure mistreatment at the hands of her supposed social betters. Occasionally the waitress will make this challenge explicit, by proclaiming emphatically that the customer cannot or should not speak to her abusively.

There was a white male. He was white. I shouldn't use the word "white," but it was a white male. . . . He came in and he was a very type hyper person looking [hyper-looking type person] to me. And he wanted a cup of coffee to go. . . . And he asked me if the manager was in . . . because he wanted to fill out an application to get hired. I replied to this man, I said, "Are you kidding? Six o'clock in the morning?" . . . He wanted to fill out an application to get a *job* at six o'clock in the morning, Greta. After he left, I'm assuming this guy felt very bad the way I approached him about the job, so he came *back*, and he said to me, "What's the matter with you? Are you stupid or something? I asked you for regular coffee," and he used the palm of his hand as the color the coffee should be. *"White.* Can't you tell *white*? . . . Don't you know, this is white, this is white? Can't you understand? Are you stupid?" And from that type of remark that he made to me, I went off. . . . With the way I am now, okay, I don't take any nonsense from no one. . . . Customers included, waitress, waiters, dishwashers, management, you name the team of Route, I don't take no junk from them, because I demand to make sure that I treat you fair, you treat me fair. . . . Had he been an intelligent person, he would not even applied himself in *person.* Let more [let alone] ask a waitress for an application at six o'clock in the morning. What a idiot. So anyway, what I did was, I said to this guy, I said, "Who in the Hell do you think you are?" . . . I told him, I said, "Don't you dare talk to me this way, cause I take this pot of

water and I throw it right into your damn face."
And I was serious, because at that moment, I felt
that I don't need this guy in here bugging me
early in the morning for a job.

Another waitress recounted the following episode that occurred after she had accidentally spilled water into the lap of a customer:

> He jumps up, he pushes me out of the way, and
> he goes, "You just blew your tip! . . . I'm going to
> have your *job!* That's what I'm going to have."
> And I turned around and looked at him. I said,
> "*Excuse* me? . . . *You're* going to have *my* job?
> *You* don't even have a job, and you're going to
> have *my* job? No. You're not going to have *my*
> job." . . . Because I don't take that. I told him, I
> said, "If you think I'm some stupid bimbo, don't
> know how to do nothing but wait tables, you're a
> *fool.* So don't even talk to me like that." . . . I
> have to tell people off . . . if they got a problem.
> When they're degrading me personally, then I
> will tell them, "I don't have to put up with your
> shit. I don't have to wait on you. I don't have to.
> You can leave."

Another waitress recalled:

> I had brought out this lady's chicken fried steak
> and the middle of it wasn't cooked enough for
> her. . . . Instead of her saying, "Ma'am, would
> you please take this back to the kitchen and have
> it cooked a little bit more?" she slide that shit
> over to me and said, "You take this shit back in the
> kitchen cause it ain't cooked." I turn around to

her, I said, "Who the Hell you think you're talking to?" I said, "Do you know who you're talking
to?" I said, "Do I look like one of your children?
Cause if I do, you better take another look. Now I
can understand that you upset cause the middle
of your chicken ain't done. . . . But. In the same
token, I think you better learn to tone that voice
of yours down. Cause you don't talk to me or
nobody else like that." "Well" [the woman said],
"I don't have to take this. I talk to the mana"— I
said, "Damn you, lady, you talk to any damn
person you want to talk to." Cause I by that time
I'd about had it. She [could] kiss my ass far as I
was concerned.

These comments illustrate the waitress's concern with
contesting the belief that a server who is rude to a customer will lose her job. The waitress who related the
incident above described the customer's view as follows:

They figure they say what they want and do what
they want; figure that you might be afraid to say
anything. . . . You know, "She ain't going to say
nothing because . . . I go to the boss and tell her
boss and she'll lose her job, so she ain't going to
say nothing to me."

When assumptions like these surface, in the form of
reckless rudeness or threats to contact supervisors, the
waitress responds by informing the customer or demonstrating by her actions that she is confident no action will
be taken against her.

The following exchange concluded a heated inter-
change between a waitress and customer regarding the
waitress's failure to remember that the customer's boy-

friend had not ordered sausage with his breakfast. Note that the waitress volunteers her name to the customer, underscoring her lack of concern with being reported (also see Nera's comments in Chapter 2).

> She [the customer] said, "Well, I would like to call in the morning and talk to your manager." I said, "Fine. My name is Mae Merrin. You can call him. I been here seven years. I ain't going nowhere. Especially over a couple pieces of meat."

Regardless of whether the waitress directly confronts the issue of her own expendability, her decision to retaliate against an offensive customer challenges the view that she, like a servant, is constrained to submit to abuse as part of her job. The promptness and intensity of her reaction indicate the degree to which this conception diverges from her own perception of self as an independent, but to the company indispensable, businessperson.

Hazards of Personality Control

Within the service sector, the process of rationalization has not been confined to the physical tasks of work. Attempts have also been made to control the personality the employee projects and the emotions she expresses. As with the physical tasks of service (making change, pouring drinks), rationalization of the worker's interactive stance is achieved by transferring control over the decisions of work from employee to service "expert." C. Wright Mills (1956:180) describes the process as it has affected salesmanship:

What he [the salesperson] says and what he can't
say is put down for him in his sales manual. . . .
His very presentation of proposition, product,
and self is increasingly given to him, increasingly
standardized and tested. Sales executives, repre-
senting the force that is centralizing and rationalizing salesmanship, have moved to the top levels
of the big companies. The brains in salesmanship,
the personal flair, have been centralized from
scattered individuals and are now managed by
those who standardize and test the presentation
which the salesmen memorize and adapt.

In the airline industry, efforts to shape the worker's projected personality begin before an individual has
been hired. A career guide for flight attendants includes a
section on mannerisms in which prospective attendants
are instructed how long to maintain eye contact and
how much enthusiasm to display during the interview
(Hochschild 1983:96). Like appearance codes, regulation
of workers' mannerisms, facial expressions, tone of voice,
and choice of words requires them to subordinate part of
themselves to company control. The intention in both
cases is to ensure that workers will convey the desired
image of the company to the public, and that this image
will elicit the desired response—satisfaction and continued patronage—from consumers.

The demand that those who serve assume a personality prescribed by their employer is not an innovation of modern service industries. In the past, a domestic's ability to present a submissive persona was
considered a more decisive determinant of his worth than
his ability to cook or serve (Sutherland 1981:37). Nor is
the need to project a false self limited to interaction
strictly defined as service. James Scott (1985:284) sug-

gests that dissimulation, and in particular the expression of false deference to those in power, is the requisite pose of all subordinate classes. Erving Goffman (1967:10) goes further, arguing that the need to maintain an expressive order consistent with one's assumed self-image or face "make[s] of every man his own jailer."

While interpersonal activity may always and everywhere have demanded maintenance of a facade, individuals are increasingly pressured to experience, rather than merely express appropriate emotions. In *The Managed Heart*, Hochschild (1983) proposes that organizations are no longer content that their workers engage in surface acting, which relies on technical maneuvers to portray feelings, and in which "the body, not the soul, is the main tool of the trade" (1983:37). Today, workers are encouraged to engage in deep or method acting, in which the worker draws on a reservoir of "emotion memories" to produce an appropriate response (empathy, cheerfulness) for a given role and scene. Toward this end, workers are urged to adopt a view of the service encounter and of the consumer that will evoke a suitable interactive stance. Flight attendants are counseled to look upon the cabin as a living room and passengers as guests, and to regard difficult passengers as children who need attention. The assumption is that flight attendants will feel sincerely sympathetic with passengers they perceive as guests or children and will not be inclined to reciprocate their anger or impatience (Hochschild 1983).

By furnishing the waitress with the script, costume, and backdrop of a servant, the restaurant encourages her to become absorbed in her role or, in Hochschild's terms, to engage in deep acting. In so doing, the company may hope to enhance the authenticity of the performance and reduce the possibility that the server will break character and express emotions incongruous with the role she is expected to play. As one who perceives herself as a servant, the waitress should willingly abdicate her claim to the courtesies of interaction between equals; she should absorb abuse with no thought of retaliation; she should fulfill requests however trivial and unreasonable, and accept blame however misdirected, because as a servant it is her job to do so.

Several researchers have commented on the potential for an individual who is subject to personality or emotion control to become estranged from her feelings, and ultimately from herself. Mills (1956:184) argues that the salesperson whose personality is transformed into an "instrument of an alien purpose" will become "self-alienated." Hochschild (1983) warns that workers whose emotions are consistently managed for commercial purposes may become estranged from their feelings, much as factory workers become estranged from their bodies. Even when emotional estrangement or detachment serves defensive functions, it is injurious, "for in dividing up our sense of self, in order to save the 'real' self from unwelcome intrusions, we necessarily relinquish a healthy sense of wholeness. We come to accept as normal the tension we feel between our 'real' and our 'on-stage' selves" (Hochschild 1983:183–84). David Riesman (1953) argues in *The Lonely Crowd* that workers who are constrained to engage in false personalization (roughly equivalent to Hochschild's "emotional labor") may lose the capacity to distinguish between coerced and genuine friendliness (1953:305).[13] Riesman identifies the demand for false personalization, with co-workers as well as consumers, as "a principal barrier to autonomy in the sphere of work" and advocates increased automatization as a means of alleviating the emotionally coercive element from the workplace (1953:302). Presumably being replaced by a machine is preferable to making an instrument of one's self.

More than anything else, the waitress's ability to

withstand the symbolic machinery of her work without suffering emotional estrangement testifies to her power of resistance. Though constrained to comply with the interactive conventions of master and servant, while clad in a domestic's uniform, the waitress does not internalize an image of service as servitude and self as servant. In times of stress she sees her work as war and herself as soldier. In times of peace she sees her work as a private enterprise and herself as entrepreneur. Like all social actors, the waitress monitors her projected personality and manipulates her feelings in the course of social interaction, but she does so knowingly and in her own interests. This manipulation of self does not induce self-alienation or emotional disorientation. The waitress distinguishes clearly between emotions expressed in order to please or appease a potential tipper, and emotions that arise spontaneously and are genuine. With experience her ability to separate front and backstage expressions of subservience and conviviality increases and she may silently applaud her powers of deception even as she stands before her audience of customers. To some extent, too, the waitress determines the degree to which she is willing to put up with rudeness in the interests of protecting a potential tip. In the terms of Hochschild's dramaturgical metaphor, she reserves the right to break character; in terms of her own idioms of war and private enterprise, she retains the right to reciprocate the aggressions of her opponents in battle and business.

Here again the intention has not been to deny that waitressing and other direct-service jobs are emotionally taxing and exploitive. Work that regularly provokes outbursts of anger and engenders an embittered view of those with whom one must daily interact, off and on the job, is both injurious and in the strictest sense, coercive. It has also not been the purpose of this discussion to exonerate organizations that perpetuate rituals of deference that threaten the dignity and deny the personhood of those who serve. Though the waitress rejects the symbolic implications of these rituals, her customers do not. The symbolism of service encourages the customer to assume the posture of master to servant, with all accompanying rights of irrationality, condescension, and unrestrained anger. The resulting conflict of perspectives is a constant source of friction between server and served, friction that diminishes the quality of the waitress's work environment and periodically erupts into open fire.

The aim of this discussion has been to explore the ways in which the waitress confronts the emotionally coercive demands of her work. Researchers of emotion-controlling labor, like many observers of women, have tended to focus on the exploitive policies of the workplace, while deemphasizing the ways in which workers respond to or protect themselves against exploitation. When the responses of women are considered at all, it is the injuries suffered that receive attention. Hochschild, for example, argues that

> the more often "tips" about how to see, feel, and seem are issued from above and the more effectively the conditions of the "stage" are kept out of the hands of the actor, the less she can influence her entrances and exits and the nature of her acting in between. The less influence she has, the more likely it is that one of two things will occur. Either she will overextend herself into the job and burn out, or she will remove herself from the job and feel bad about it. (1983:189)

Route waitresses demonstrate that women may respond to the adverse conditions of their work not merely in the

passive sense of suffering injuries, but by actively resisting, reformulating, or rejecting the coercive forces
they encounter. Like the flight attendant, the waitress is
pressured to see and feel about her work in company-
endorsed ways; and like the flight attendant, she has little
influence over the setting of the stage on which she must
act out her work role. And yet the waitress does not
overextend herself into her work, and when she distances
herself from her job she does not "feel bad about it."

Analysts of emotion labor may have been led to
deemphasize the ways in which women respond to the
hazards of their work by the often silent or hidden nature
of women's resistance. The waitress sometimes breaks
character and rejects the role of servant, but for the most
part her resistance is unseen, taking place behind a facade of subservience or behind the lines, out of sight of
customers. What remains to be determined is why those
who serve do not more often openly reject the degrading
symbolism of servitude. Scott provides a possible answer.

> Open insubordination in almost any context will
> provoke a more rapid and ferocious response than
> an insubordination that may be as pervasive but
> never ventures to contest the formal definitions
> of hierarchy and power. For most subordinate
> classes, which, as a matter of sheer history, have
> had little prospect of improving their status, this
> form of resistance has been the only option. What
> may be accomplished *within* this symbolic strait-
> jacket is nonetheless something of a testament to
> human persistence and inventiveness. (1985:33)

The truth of this statement is demonstrated in those
instances in which waitresses do contest the formal definition of hierarchy and power and engage in open in-

subordination. Customers who find their anger reciprocated by a waitress typically respond with intensified
displays of anger or ominous demands to see the manager. Contrary to customer belief, the waitress is not
liable to lose her job or be censured as a result of her
defiance. In truth, the manager is likely to express sympathy with the waitress, to apologize to her for the customers' misconduct, and to join with her in verbally dis-
paraging the departed party. Still, the waitress's defiance
is damaging to her. In withdrawing from the role of servant by retaliating against abusive customers or informing them that they cannot "degrade" her, the waitress
releases them from their obligation to fulfill the requirements of their role as customers. In short, she provides
them with a license to stiff. For this reason, and not for
fear she will lose her job, the waitress strives to suppress
her anger and her negative views of the public behind a
mask of subservience. Silent resistance may not be the
only option open to her, but it is the most profitable.

An alternative explanation for the apparent compliance of women to exploitive or demeaning conditions
is provided by Shirley Ardener.

> While professing to support the values and codes
> of behaviour embodied in the dominant system,
> perhaps their own sense of value derives from a
> muted counterpart system, of which they may
> not themselves even be completely aware. For
> instance, the principal measure for social success
> or for other satisfactions in the counterpart model
> may differ from that of the model of the dominant
> group, and therefore their acquiescence at being
> placed low down on the latter's scale for success
> may occur because the placing seems unimpor-
> tant or irrelevant to them, since they may not

necessarily be 'unsuccessful' or 'unsatisfied' according to the logic of their own muted model. (1975:xvii)

In the waitress's counterpart model she is not a servant, but an independent businessperson or a soldier. Success and satisfaction in these occupations are predicated on the individual's ability to control the behavior of those with whom she enters into business transactions or does battle. By upholding the symbolic order and complying with the rituals of servitude, the waitress, as businessperson, achieves success in the form of greater tip income. As soldier, the waitress achieves success by refusing to let enemy fire penetrate her facade; by deflecting the aggressions of her opponents with a shield of stoicism.

7

Conclusion

If you come to Route on Sunday morning you will find a crowd of customers at the door and several parties congregated at the register waiting to pay their checks. Those who are arriving exchange sardonic comments with those who are leaving about the speed of service, and everyone wonders why there is no one to seat people or take their money. Eventually a hostess will arrive, looking flustered and keeping her eyes lowered as she works the register, to avoid the impatient stares of other customers. A man in a suit clears dirty plates and glasses from a booth by the window, bending over to scrape a piece of pancake off the booth bench before wiping it with a rag. A waitress bursts full speed from the kitchen and heads toward the floor, carrying eight steaming plates on her left arm, another two in her right hand, and a bottle of catsup in one pocket. She weaves between the customers milling around the register, swinging her arms upward to avoid collision with the children who race across her path and calling out "behind you!" when she crosses behind other waitresses. As she passes the man in the suit—who is her manager—she stops and turns her hip slightly toward him. Without looking up from his load of dirty plates, he slips the tip from the booth into her empty pocket and continues to clear the table.

If you follow the waitress as she delivers her orders and makes her rounds on the floor, you will find that her customers are often irritable and impolite to her. They do not acknowledge her when she approaches the table to take an order to refill coffee, and when she speaks they cut her off to complain that their food is over- or underdone, is not what they wanted, or is taking too long. You will find that the waitress is constantly running, lifting, loading and unloading dishes, and receiving little assistance in the performance of her job duties. The dollars and change she picks up from her empty tables may seem to you to be paltry compensation for her exertions.

If you now follow the waitress behind the partition which conceals the kitchen region from the sensitive eye of the public, you will encounter an environment very different from the front house. Here there are no carpets, no potted plants, no piped-in golden oldies. The tile floor is greasy and wet, making it difficult to maintain your footing without holding the wall for support. The counters are littered with half-empty glasses of milk and juice, half-peeled bananas, dirty silverware, and melting ice. Four or five women crowd against the counter under the cooks' window, anxiously watching events on the pass bar, which is piled high with orders, and on the line, where four cooks in stained white smocks pivot between flaming burners, spitting grills, and churning deep fryers, pausing only to wipe the sweat out of their eyes. Some waitresses stand on tiptoe and strain to reach plates that have just been put up; others shout through the window that they are missing orders of bacon, returning rejected omelettes, and reordering toast and hash browns. Their voices can barely be heard over the racket of banging dishes and the shouting of others around them. New waitresses rush in from the floor, scribbling in their books as they come, while those who have just put checks in dash from counter to counter pouring drinks and gathering pitchers of syrup, dishes of jelly, and bowls of cereal. Nobody flinches when a plate of scrambled eggs slips off the counter and shatters, or when the coffeepot boils over onto the floor. Restaurant workers are accustomed to chaos.

The waitresses are hot, tired, and many of them are visibly angry. As they wait for orders to come up or stack plates to go out, they complain about the ineptitude of management and the stupidity and rudeness of their customers. Several hint that they are approaching the breaking point and are ready to walk out. Their vehemence contrasts strangely with the girlish, maid's aprons they wear as uniforms, and with the cheerful countenance some assume as they turn away from the kitchen and return to the floor.

From this glimpse of Route on a busy Sunday morning, you will probably conclude that the waitress's work is dirty and demeaning, and you will wonder what motivates her to endure this thankless occupation. You might ask whether she finds anything positive to recommend her work; whether she strives to improve the conditions of her labor in some way; and if she aspires to move up from the floor one day. You might also wonder how the manager responds to the frustration of his employees, why he is bussing the waitresses' tables, and how this job fits in with his role as a supervisor and administrator. These are some of the questions and issues this work has hoped to address.

Structure and Strategy

This investigation has found the work of the waitress to bear all the outer markings of a traditional female occupation. Each detail of the work process is regulated by the company; job tasks center on the performance of traditional female duties: serving, waiting, smiling, flattering; and emphasize putatively female qualities: patience, sociability, submissiveness; and there are no meaningful opportunities to advance. The symbolism of service involves the waitress in daily rituals of subservience, which underscore her subordination to those she serves and identify her as a member of a historically disparaged class of servants. Wages are low and she is compelled to rely on an inherently unstable source for the bulk of her income. It is not surprising that such a system of compensation is the trademark of an occupation dominated by women, for women have generally been viewed as secondary earners. It is presumed that fluctuations in their earnings will affect the family's luxury expenditures but will not compromise its financial stability.

The waitress has little chance of fundamentally altering the structural constraints of her work. The tipping system is a ubiquitous and entrenched feature of the food service industry, which she can reject only by rejecting her chosen vocation. The symbols and conventions of service have survived the transition from an industrial to postindustrial society and can be expected to persevere through future transformations of the labor market. The downgrading of the managerial role, which has rendered advancement meaningless in the restaurant, is in large part the product of a process of centralization that has been in operation since the inception of scientific management in the last decades of the nineteenth century (Braverman 1974). The same deep-rooted process underlies the extensive campaign to rationalize the waitress's job tasks, her personal appearance, and her interactive stance.

Nonetheless, the waitress is not a passive casualty

of the hardships of her work. Within the structural parameters of her job she has developed an arsenal of often subtle but undeniably effective tactics to moderate the exploitive elements of her occupation and secure attention to her needs. The organizational structure of the restaurant influences how she defines her work interests and shapes the strategies she employs in their defense. In transferring control over her income to the public, for instance, the tipping system motivates the waitress to focus her energies on cultivating the favor of customers, not management. Accordingly, she sacrifices company policy and interests to the needs of her parties, providing them with extra and oversized portions of whatever she can obtain without the assistance of cooks, and occasionally failing to charge for desserts or drinks. At the same time she works to maximize the overall number of gratuities she receives by circumventing the customer rotation system, concentrating on turning her tables, and neglecting to offer particularly troublesome or time-consuming items that might slow the overall speed of her service.

In contrast to financially dependent employees, the waitress does not feel constrained to impress her manager with her punctuality, her enthusiasm, or her devotion. She does not indulge his ego by admiring his wisdom, his judgment, or his wit. On the contrary, she ignores his occasional appeals for sympathy and openly confronts him with his faults, telling him he is "unprofessional" or just "a jerk," and accentuating her anger by throwing her order book. As a quasi-independent businessperson, she defines her obligations toward the company narrowly: work that does not directly contribute to her tip earnings is carried out reluctantly or neglected; tasks performed primarily for management's benefit are regarded as favors which place the recipient in the grant-

or's debt. Thus, while the waitress does not directly challenge the tipping system, she has resolved that as long as
the company does not take responsibility for her financial
welfare, it will not lay claim to her loyalty, or command
her obedience without providing alternative remunera-
tion.

Our study indicates that the waitress maintains
considerable control over the work process, despite the
company's efforts to rationalize the delivery of service.
Here too, structural factors of the restaurant industry
contribute to her ability to enhance her position; but,
the control she enjoys is not merely or entirely a given of
her occupation. Rather, it is achieved through the active
and in some cases conscious manipulation of conditions
that create the possibility of control. Features of the
waitress's work environment that enable her to protect
her autonomy include inadequate training and chronic
shortages of supplies and support staff, which compel her
to employ creative problem solving in stress situations
and furnish her with justification for confiscating autonomy in other contexts; the irregular pace of restaurant
work, which creates slow periods that servers use as they
please, possibly in return for forgoing formal breaks; the
organization of the serving process, in which the waitress
performs most tasks of service herself, allowing her to
regulate the pace and decisions of her work in accordance
with her own standards and conceptions of efficiency; and
the labor crisis that reduces the risk of firing or prolonged
unemployment. We have also found that the waitress
exploits the manager's position as fill-in man in a labor-
hungry industry to expand the boundaries of her control.
Aware that the manager must compensate for absent
employees with his own time and labor, she strategically
concludes her demands for greater freedom or consideration with the ultimatum, "Either you, . . . or I'm leav-

ing." Should the manager fail to meet the terms of this ultimatum she may execute her threat, leaving behind half-made desserts, half-taken orders, food in the window, checks on the wheel, and a station full of expectant customers.

Perhaps the waitress's greatest victory is her success in insulating herself against the psychological hazards of her work. Her methods of self-protection in this domain are not consciously developed or implemented, but grow out of and reflect the distinctive challenges of her work. Many of the pressures she faces are subtle and symbolic; so, too, are her methods of defense. She extricates herself from the coercive symbolism of service, countering company-backed and customer-supported images of servitude with her own metaphors of war and entrepreneurship. She inverts the symbolism of a bad tip, transforming it from a statement on her work skills or low status into evidence of the ignorance or cheapness of the customer. Customers do not treat her as an individual entitled to the courtesies of polite interaction; she in turn denies their personhood, treating them as inanimate material to be processed quickly and dispassionately in view of extracting a tip. They address her by first name, or hail her indecorously with a wave of the hand and a "Miss!"; she reciprocates the compliment, by referring to them as tables or numbers, which are *turned, coffeed, watered,* or *picked up*—not served. They regard her as a member of an incompetent and lazy class of servants; she sees them as part of an inherently hostile public and categorizes them within a customer typology according to their specific character deficiencies. The waitress's preference for silent resistance is not merely a reflection of the subtlety of the challenges she faces, nor is it a symptom of timidity. By cognitively repudiating the customer's status as master, while outwardly supporting the symbolic order, the waitress nurtures the pride and stimulates the generosity of those who provide the greater part of her income. She manipulates herself to manipulate the other to her financial advantage.

On some occasions the waitress forsakes silent resistance in favor of open confrontation. If a party's demands are too rigorous or its complaints too severe, she reserves the right to challenge its misuse and in some instances to terminate the encounter by refusing further service. In so doing she forfeits the prospect of a favorable gratuity, but it is she who decides whether the gain in dignity counterbalances the monetary loss. Once again, structural factors of the restaurant provide necessary, but not sufficient, conditions for the waitress to defend her interests. Because her conversations with customers take place out of earshot of management, and because managers are reluctant to exacerbate their labor problems by imposing negative sanctions on employees, it is possible for the waitress to confront rude customers without fear of negative repercussions from her employer. For a confrontation to take place, however, the waitress must first resolve that it is her right to determine how much she will endure from those she serves, and she must possess the spirit of defiance—and the gumption—needed to stand her ground against customers who regard impatience, condescension, and unrestrained hostility as their natural rights.

Structural elements of the restaurant industry also play a role in determining the methods the waitress does not adopt to improve her position. The waitress's lack of interest in unionization can be partly attributed to the individualistic ethos of the restaurant, which is encouraged by a system of compensation in which co-workers must compete against each other to maximize their incomes. Aggressive individualism is fostered by the structure of the waitress's job, which allows her to conduct her work independently of the concerns, needs, or habits of her co-workers; by supply shortages, which force workers to vie for resources critical to the efficient execution of their work; and by the demarcation of the restaurant floor into stations, with its associated emphasis on maintaining the property and territorial rights of workers. The waitress's code of noninterference, itself an outgrowth of her image of self as entrepreneur and ultimately of her financial independence as a tipped employee, further mitigates against a collective spirit, as any attempt at coordinated action could be regarded as a violation of the server's right to sovereignty in the performance of her work.

The waitress's lack of concern with moving up is, likewise, a function of structural parameters of the restaurant: in this case a reward structure that bears little relationship to the structure of advancement. Within the restaurant, promotion to the managerial ranks is rewarded by long hours, low pay, increased responsibility, and vulnerability to undependable and sometimes vengeful employees. In order to keep the restaurant functioning under the pressure of the labor crisis, the manager is forced to spend his work hours washing dishes and playing hostess and is compelled to put in extensive overtime for which, as a salaried employee, he is not compensated. The power and authority traditionally associated with his role have been narrowly circumscribed by a dual process of centralization and routinization, which deprives him of decision-making power over the most trivial details of his work. Given these conditions, waitresses have little motivation to advance, and they devote their energies instead to augmenting the advantages of their current position.

The relationship between the structural constraints of the restaurant and the waitress's protective strategies reminds us of the range of forms that action is likely to take. The structure of an occupation necessarily influences how the worker perceives and protects her needs: central concerns in one context may be peripheral issues in another; resistance that is effective in one setting will be self-defeating or inappropriate under a different set of pressures and limitations. If we overlook or undervalue the bond between structure and strategy and implicitly generalize the concerns and behaviors of one segment of the work force, we will inevitably be led to the conclusion that many workers are unable to protect or even recognize their best interests. In our case, reliance on bureaucratic concepts of career advancement or industrial models of protest might lead us to interpret the waitress's disinterest in mobility as passivity and her failure to unionize as apathy. By examining the waitress's choices and strategies of action in the context of the distinctive constraints of the food service industry, however, we have discovered that the waitress's rejection of promotion opportunities is well motivated by the distribution of rewards in the restaurant and that, while she does not engage in collective action, she has found other ways to manipulate her work environment to serve her needs.

The Significance of Autonomy

Many of the waitress's strategies of action are, at root, efforts to expand and protect her autonomy. In resisting the pervasive metaphor of servitude, she fights to retain control over her subjective state: to determine how she perceives herself, her customers, and the relationship between them. In reciprocating the rudeness of antagonistic customers she asserts her right to emotional

sovereignty: the right to draw the limits of her own tolerance and retaliate when these limits are transgressed. In
diverting a disproportionate number of customers to her
tables, declining to wait on poor tippers, and striving to
secure the most lucrative stations for herself, she claims
the right to control her income, refusing to be the victim
of an unreliable system of compensation. In declining
opportunities to advance, she seeks to retain control over
the decisions of her work and maintain her freedom from
the obligations of the financially dependent employee.

The waitress's concern with autonomy is consistent with research on work attitudes that identifies autonomy or control as a critical component of job satisfaction
(Blauner 1969). Robert Blauner (1969:233) suggests that
the worker's need for control may be a consequence of
the emphasis on "individual initiative" in American culture, but this does not explain the equally strong need for
autonomy exhibited by workers in other countries (see,
for instance, Mercure, Regimbald, and Tanguay 1987).
Fred Katz (1968) proposes that autonomy, however limited, may serve to compensate low-ranking employees for
the otherwise meager rewards of their work. Factory
workers have little control over the pace and decisions of
their job tasks but enjoy some freedom in areas not directly related to work performance. They are allowed to
import features of their working-class culture (practical
joking, verbal play, "prankish physical contact") into the
work context, though these features are antithetical to
the company's ethos. Katz (1968:53) suggests that such
structurally guaranteed spheres of autonomy "can be
viewed as part of the exchange (in addition to monetary
pay) for the limited forms of reward and participation that
the worker is given by the employing organization."

The finding that waitresses are willing to walk off
a shift or quit rather than yield to interference in their

work supports the hypothesis that autonomy binds low-ranking employees to their jobs. Women in particular may value autonomy on the job because they have been deprived of control in other areas, or at other times of their lives. Lillian Rubin's (1976) study of working-class families reveals that husbands control all important decisions within the household, including some relating to issues traditionally understood as the province of the wife. Rubin believes that men may feel a special need to exert authority at home, and that women may honor this need, because as assembly-line workers and laborers in refineries, men have no voice, no influence in the workplace.[1]

As a corollary to Rubin's hypothesis it might be suggested that waitresses and other working-class women manifest a desire for autonomy at work because they are excluded from decision making and denied a voice in the home. In some cases the need for control may derive from past experiences of powerlessness as much as current power relations in the home.

> When I was younger, we were homeless. When I was a little girl. . . . It was more or less my father's fault . . . because he would uproot us from house to house and we would live in cars and motels, but he *chose* to do that. He *always* argued with my mother about money, money, money. He could never get enough money. That's why money doesn't mean that much to me, because it shows me the evilness in people and what it does to people. It's Satan in other words.

Subjected as a child to the control of a father who chose to uproot her family from motel to house to car, this waitress may feel a particular need to resist control in adulthood. Interestingly, she is known in the restaurant for not caring whether she gets her rightful share of customers, and hence tips: an attitude that supports her stated indifference to money.

At the other end of the spectrum, Nera, well known for being money hungry, attributes her demanding approach to work to memories of her parents' life of sharecropping.

> We come home, we count our money, because we're a waitress, and we can say, "I made X amount of dollars." Well, when you're sharecropping . . . you don't see any of your money until the end of the year. . . . The people owns the land, will provide you . . . all the things that would need to keep your farming in good condition . . . but there is a record that is kept. . . . And from that record at the end of the year, once you take your tobacco out to be sold, once you finish picking all your cotton, once you taken all your peanuts . . . whatever the total amount is . . . all the credit that [my father] had all during the year . . . had to pay off all these things, before you could say you cleared anything. Sometime, after working all year long, you may clear a thousand dollars. So you know, now you see I'm like a very forward, demanding type person. It's because you will learn not to let people use you.

Nera, who came to New York at eighteen to escape a life of sharecropping, went on to recall the treatment she received at the employment agency that had paid her busfare North.

> I went into the agency office, and there's all these rich white people . . . rich, rich, powerful people that come into this agency that is . . . using an ad to get blacks to the North so they can charge the

rich people a big fee . . . to bring them [blacks] to their homes [as servants]. . . . Women with the cigarette with the holder, smoking . . . politician wives. . . . Eighty-five percent of the people [blacks] that was in that office could not read nor write. . . . I was one of the lucky ones that could. . . . So when I was interviewed, this one lady called me up . . . she said, "Turn around." Just like you see slavery days. "Turn around." Okay? "Turn around." I turned around. And she said, "Well Mr. Jones . . . is looking for someone to just perhaps . . . cook breakfast . . . uh two children, uh yes, turn around, turn around." And you're standing there like this. . . . Had I known like I know today, you understand what I'm saying, *no one* would ever ask *me* to turn *my* body around so they can determine whether or not I look to be strong enough, to be educated enough to even allow myself to go into their home to say, "Yes, I'll change your baby's diapers for you."

Observing Nera at Route it is difficult to imagine her ever submitting to this degrading exercise. Her refusal to "take any nonsense from no one" and her quickness to confront managers on issues of unfair treatment have earned her a reputation for an iron will and helped her build a strong power base within the restaurant. Memories of powerlessness and ill treatment, such as that recounted here, may intensify Nera's resistance to interference and loss of control in her current work life, as memories of sharecropping conduce to her concern with getting her fair share (and sometimes more) of customers. For Nera, and for other women who have felt the pain of powerlessness in other spheres or at other times of their lives, autonomy at work may be valued more strongly and guarded more closely, not because it is perceived as an inviolable human right, but because experience has proven that it is not.

The autonomy the waitress wins for herself is rare and valuable at a time when we are increasingly pressured to regulate our subjective states as well as our schedules and work habits to conform to the demands of the workplace. It is especially surprising to find this level of autonomy in a female-dominated occupation, because women's work outside the home has tended to be tightly regulated and lacking in opportunities for independent thought and action. It may be that the waitress is an anomaly; that her ability to defend her autonomy is the product of a confluence of factors unique to the time and place in which she works. It is also possible that women in other traditional female occupations have found ways to shield themselves from the hardships of their work and confiscate control over some aspects of their jobs, but that their methods of self-protection have been overlooked by observers who concentrate on the limiting and exploitive processes of the workplace, deemphasizing the ways in which women seek to adapt to the constraints of their position.

The strategies of working-class women may be further overlooked because they do not conform to the investigator's understanding of what constitutes resistance. Scott (1985:292) has noted a general tendency among students of the working class to limit the definition of resistance to action that is organized, cooperative, and selfless, thereby excluding from consideration the informal, often hidden "garden variety" resistance, which has typified the history of subordinate groups (1985:241). In concentrating on women's failure to engage in methods of organized, cooperative action such as unionization, observers may have failed to take notice of the types of informal and by no means selfless strategies of action, which have been examined here.

As a consequence of the bias for formal, collective action, and the focus on structural inequity and exploitation, women have frequently been perceived or implicitly portrayed as resigned to their subjection (Paules 1990a). Such a portrayal is dangerous because it hints at traditional images of women as creatures of the hearth who are largely indifferent to their work-force status. This perception undermines critiques of exploitive processes, for if it is determined that women acquiesce to the conditions of their labor, there can be no cry of oppression, no call for reform. In contrast, evidence that women have developed ways to circumvent and subvert, if not directly modify, the constraints of their work, strengthens the case for structural reform, for once we have established that women are concerned to improve their position, we can no longer claim that they condone an inequitable status quo.

This investigation has sought to avoid the view that women are resigned to their subjection by examining structure and strategy as interlocking systems, adopting a more comprehensive understanding of action, and reformulating conventional questions about women and work. Rather than ask, *Why don't women advance?* we have asked, *What motivations might women have to resist advancement?* Rather than ask, *Why are women passive?* we have asked, *How are they active?* In adopting this approach the intent has not been to downplay the difficulties of the waitress's position or deny the need for structural reform that would ensure her greater financial security and eliminate the coercive symbolism of service. Rather, the goal has been to balance pervasive images of female submission and passivity with a glimpse of defiance.

Conclusion

Implications for the Study of Men
in Low-Status Occupations

The waitress's success in manipulating her work environment to promote her interests helps to dismantle conceptions of women as passive. Her experience may also lead us to reevaluate our perceptions of working-class men, and in particular, the interpretations we place on their orientations toward advancement.

Researchers of working-class men, like researchers of women, have tended to attribute low upward mobility to shortcomings of workers rather than the jobs they reject or fail to obtain. This analytic predisposition may reflect a belief in the insufficient motivation, ambition, and ability of working-class men as well as an unchallenged confidence in the intrinsic value of advancement. This confidence may in turn derive from the assumption that whatever middle-class men have traditionally had, including the opportunity to move up, is by definition desirable.

The inclination to accept advancement as good, by definition, is clearly expressed in the research on career aspirations of automobile workers. Sociological investigations have revealed that employees in automobile factories, whose work is painfully tedious and dull, nonetheless express little interest in promotion to foremanship.[2] Robert Guest's study of experienced factory workers found that

> interestingly enough, the overwhelming majority [of workers who expressed a desire to change jobs] *held their aspirations down* to other blue-collar jobs, and only 7 per cent expressed the desire to become supervisors. (1954:157–58; emphasis added)

Conclusion

In a similar tone of puzzlement, E. Wight Bakke remarks:

> Inasmuch as a foremanship was the highest status in the shop to which most workers might aspire, it was a bit surprising to find a rather general lack of enthusiasm for such promotion. . . . It is probably a fortunate condition that men shall not aspire too frequently to jobs they can not hope to acquire in view of the large numbers of men compared with the paucity of the jobs. (1969:51–52)

Of the sixty-two men interviewed by Ely Chinoy,

> only five . . . expressed any real hope of ever becoming foremen. While seven others had given up the hopes they had once had, fifty said that they would not want to be foremen or that they had never thought of the possibility. (1952:455)

Chinoy (1952:455) comments that his findings are consistent with Bakke's and with a poll of factory workers conducted by *Fortune* (1947) "in which 58 per cent of the sample said that they would not care to be foremen."

In explaining their lack of enthusiasm for foremanship, auto workers point to the same drawbacks described by waitresses in connection with management. Foremanship is said to entail "too much responsibility," "too much grief," exposure to the tyranny of higher-level management, and vulnerability to disgruntled workers who can cause "accidents," which slow output in the foreman's department (Chinoy 1955:58–59). In addition, auto workers feel that promotion to foremanship would transform work into an "unpleasant duty" and involve the performance of unprincipled acts, such as squealing (Bakke 1969:52). Finally, as Chinoy (1952:455) points out, foremanship "rarely leads to better managerial posts," and for skilled workers at least, would not entail a significant increase in income (1955:59).

Though seemingly straightforward, these explanations are invariably brushed aside by researchers intent to discover the "true" source of the auto worker's deficient ambition. Bakke (1969:52) grants that indifference to promotion should not be regarded as "merely a case of a rationalized failure," then goes on to interpret the workers' negative appraisal of foremanship as evidence that they do not wish "to control *others*." Despite his initial disclaimer, Bakke ends by attributing the disparagement of advancement to shortcomings of the worker: his lack of concern with controlling others or, more plainly, his inadequate drive for power. Chinoy admits that foremanship may have a down side, and that "in many cases" disinterest in foremanship may be "genuine," but concentrates his analysis on the hypothesis that the disparagement of advancement represents a "defensive cover-up to blunt one's guilt over not getting ahead or over the failure to sustain the ambition so strongly encouraged by tradition" (1955:57). The researcher thus manages to find in the worker's rejection of advancement, evidence that advancement is desired. The more parsimonious (and logical) explanation—that the supervisory role is rejected because it has little to offer—is given only passing consideration.

The language used in these analyses presupposes the benefits of upward mobility and precludes impartial evaluation of alternative perspectives. Foremanship is referred to as an "escape hatch" from the rank and file; promotions are something to be "gained," occupational immobility is "failure to move up," interest in foremanship constitutes an "aspiration," and interest in blue-collar jobs represents a "holding down" of aspirations. Ambitions other than advancement are dismissed as "modest objectives," "small ambitions," and "small goals." Even ostensibly worthwhile goals such as securing a job that is "easier, steadier, or more interesting" are dismissed as "small gains" (Chinoy 1952:457), while the worker's wish to win "more individual control over work pace," and his desire to obtain a job that he can continue to perform as he grows older are strangely dismissed as "short-run and immediate" concerns (Guest 1954:163). The worker's concern with job security and his children's future, and his aspirations to go into business for himself, are classified as substitute or compensatory goals for his failure to achieve vertical mobility.

In insisting on the advantages of moving up and denying the value of alternative objectives, these researchers accuse auto workers of suffering from inadequate ambition and another working-class affliction: false consciousness, or "adhering to beliefs damaging to their interests" (Parenti 1978:15). Often, the truth or falseness of a people's consciousness is determined by the degree to which it coincides with the ideology of the observer. Apparent contentment with conditions the observer defines as exploitive is a sure sign that one suffers from false consciousness, while revolt against these conditions reflects enlightenment or "true" consciousness. The automobile worker does not rebel against the inequity of limited advancement opportunities, but takes refuge in the damaging illusion that foremanship is not worth striving for and in the pursuit of such small and short-term goals as security, control, independence, and a better future for the next generation.

It is not necessary to diagnose factory workers with false consciousness or invoke complex psychological theories of rationalization in order to explain their views on mobility. Though the possibility is rarely given serious consideration, it is conceivable that the workers' disinterest in advancement is motivated by an accurate appraisal of what foremanship has to offer. This is not to argue that opportunity flourishes in the automobile factory, or that life on the assembly line is gratifying. The point is, rather, that entry-level managerial positions, in the factory as in the restaurant, may no longer represent a clear improvement over wage-level work. It is not that waiting tables or tending an assembly line is pleasant and fulfilling, but that acting as fill-in men and middle men is no better, and in some cases worse.

It is important to distinguish the argument made here from the relativist argument, which posits alternative value systems as the source of working-class and female immobility or passivity. The line between exploitive conservatism and enlightened relativism is tangled and thin. Relativism that explains (condones) an oppressive status quo will often be exposed as a front for traditionalism. The theory that women fail to succeed at work because they value domestic fulfillment over occupational achievement is an example of traditionalism (thinly) disguised as relativism. The argument made here is not a relativist argument. It has not been suggested that the values of waitresses and factory workers differ from those of the hegemonic culture; that these workers reject advancement because they do not esteem what advancement is supposed to offer. Waitresses and factory workers may value power, prestige, and bigger paychecks as highly as middle-class men; they simply do not believe these benefits are to be obtained through promotion. Indeed, it is precisely because they value these rewards that workers at the bottom may refuse to move "up."[3]

This study of waitresses has challenged the uncritical equation of advancement with success, demonstrating the need for future research to investigate the nature and worth of higher-order jobs before seeking to determine what deficiency of opportunity, ability, or ambition prevents workers from moving up. Future research must also acknowledge that alternative strategies for improving one's work-force position exist, and that in some cases immobility may itself represent a strategy to protect the advantages of one's current position. In many instances it will be found that, in fact, the significant rewards of work pivot on mobility, and that insufficient opportunity or ability impedes the career progress of some workers. This appears to be the case, for example, in corporate environments such as that investigated by Kanter (1977). In other cases it will be found that women and other low-ranking workers remain immobile, not because they are intellectually, psychologically, or otherwise unable to advance, nor because mobility is blocked by discrimination or absence of opportunity, but because jobs higher up are no longer perceived as worth moving up into. To the extent that advancement is rewarded by longer hours and lower pay, and to the degree that first-line managers have been marginalized from the decision-making process and reduced to "servants of decisions" handed down from above, these perceptions cannot be dismissed as misperceptions. For those on the lower rungs, the ladder to the top may in fact be crooked; the road to success may no longer lead up.

Notes

Chapter 1. Introduction

1. In compliance with the American Anthropological Association's (1983) commitment to protecting the privacy of informants, names of persons, and of places that could potentially identify the restaurant, have all been replaced with pseudonyms. Information about Route that would clearly distinguish it from other restaurants has been omitted.

2. *The floor:* that part of the restaurant where booths and tables are located. To be *on the floor* is to be on duty, waiting tables. To be *off the floor* is to be no longer taking orders. A waitress who is physically on the floor may say she is off the floor to indicate that her shift is over or nearly over and she is not taking new parties.

3. *Turnover:* the succession of one party by the next at each table. The speed of turnover depends on the speed of service and on how long customers remain at the table after eating. Turnover is fast on day shift because breakfast is quickly prepared and consumed, whereas dinner takes longer to cook and can involve three or more courses. Customers are also more inclined to dawdle over

dinner, sip coffee, smoke cigarettes, talk, and digest. Turnover on grave is more erratic. Sometimes a party will occupy the same table for hours; other parties rush in for a milk shake en route to a movie.

4. *Stiffing:* nontipping (see Chapter 2).

Walkout: a party leaves the restaurant without paying the check. Occasionally refers to customers leaving before they are seated or before they order or receive their food.

5. In keeping with the sex composition of job categories at Kendelport Route at the time of research, the masculine is used in this work to refer to managers, dishwashers, and usually cooks; the feminine is used to refer to waitresses/servers and hostesses; and the terms *waitress* and *hostess* are used rather than *waiter* and *host*. In those cases where a sex-indefinite, third-person singular pronoun is needed, as for *the worker,* the feminine is used. Since in the majority of cases, *the worker* refers here to waitresses, it seems more reasonable to use *she/her*—though an occasional *he* will be subsumed under this heading—than to use *he* and so subsume the majority of female subjects under a masculine pronoun. In later chapters, first-line factory supervisors are referred to as males, and the terms *foreman* and *foremanship* are retained, because these are the terms used in the studies discussed, and because these studies deal specifically with fore*men*.

6. *Waitresses' station:* area partitioned off from the main floor, in which bus pans and garbage cans are kept, along with coffeepots, tea, silverware, napkins, and other supplies. Groups of booths and tables worked by individual waitresses are also known as stations.

7. *Up:* ready to be served.

8. The waitress's lack of concern with unionization is mirrored in this investigation: no attempt is made

to explain why waitresses do not organize, and waitresses were not, with one exception, asked how they felt about unions. To devote this analysis to determining why waitresses do not organize would be to admit the privileged status of unionization as a strategy for action and to divert attention from alternative forms of action. More important, it would artificially introduce an issue that—to judge by their silence on the topic—has little meaning for waitresses themselves. In the single instance in which I broached the subject of unionization at the restaurant to a waitress (who belonged to a union at a factory where she was also employed), the waitress responded simply that she did not feel a union would be in the interests of the company right now and went on to suggest that the district manager should instead inaugurate a headwaitress, "a leader, a person that can actually get out there and can actually get something done through the people." (It was clear from the broader context of this statement that the waitress had herself in mind for the position.) Given that interviews were confidential (informants were assured their names would not be used) and usually took place in my home or the home of the informant, and given that in general waitresses did not hesitate to voice their opinions and concerns (however much these threatened their rapport with management), it is unlikely that their silence concerning unions arose from fear of censure.

9. These figures refer to average membership for the two-year periods ending 1983 and June 30, 1987, respectively.

10. While expansion of the service sector has been greatest in the United States, Western European countries are also experiencing greater growth of services relative to goods-production (Channon 1978; Fuchs 1968; Gershuny and Miles 1983).

11. We shall find, however, that service has re-

ceived much notice from corporate strategists and journalists.

12. See, for instance, Applebaum (1984), Krause (1971), and Rothman (1987).

13. Though it is not counted as part of the formal investigation, I waitressed on and off for five years prior to commencing observations at Route. I have worked part and full time, and have waited tables on the West and East Coasts.

14. All quotes attributed to Route informants are taken from transcriptions of interviews. False starts, habit phrases ("you know," "basically," "like," "I said"), digressions, and repetitions have been deleted for clarity and brevity. Where possible, the omission of digressions and repetitions has been indicated by ellipsis points. Nothing has been deleted from the transcripts that would alter the tone or intent of an informant's comments; no words have been added without the use of brackets, and, with the exception of pseudonyms, no words have been changed.

Chapter 2. "Getting" and "Making" a Tip

1. *Call-out:* an employee calls the restaurant to say she will not be coming to work because of sickness, transportation problems, or a personal emergency. Employees often call out shortly before they are supposed to start work, or after their scheduled shift has begun, making it difficult for management to find replacements in time.

2. *Front house:* area of restaurant open to customers, including the floor, the register and waiting area, and the customer restrooms. The *back house* comprises all areas to which the public does not have access, includ-

ing the kitchen, dish room, managers' office, stockroom, main waitresses' station, and employee break room and restrooms. To *run the front house* is primarily to perform the duties of hostess, though the expression carries supervisory connotations.

3. *Pick up:* to take the order from or wait on a party.

4. For a discussion of possible sources of the discrepancy between these observations and past interpretations of how workers view poor tips, see Paules 1990a.

5. At Route, *stiff* is used most commonly as a verb ("I got stiffed"), and as a noun only to refer to the incident of being stiffed ("I had four stiffs"), not to the customers themselves. Nonetheless, the use of *stiff* to refer directly to the customer is reported by Donovan (1920) and is listed in current slang dictionaries, indicating that its loss may be recent or that its use may be confined to regions of the country other than the Northeast. The fact that waitresses at Route do not refer to customers as stiffs is consistent with their tendency to deemphasize the status of customers as autonomous selves (for instance, through the use of objectifying terminology).

6. This waitress's response should not be interpreted as a manifestation of racial hostility. She adopted the same defiant pose toward difficult white customers and was herself married to an African-American man and the loving mother of an African-American son. Nonetheless, there was racial tension of various kinds at Route. Some servers, for example, felt that African-American young adults tended to be poor tippers and ill-mannered, and thus disliked waiting on them, and some African-American waitresses felt that white waitresses received preferential treatment from managers including, apparently, a manager who was himself African American. One

waitress commented that "when a white waitress do something [wrong], it's like, 'Oh, it was a mistake. . . .' But if you let a black one start doing the same thing . . . they make the show [an example] of the black one." My impression was that management did favor white waitresses somewhat, but primarily those who were, in the words of the informant quoted above, "pretty . . . blond hair, blue eyes, or very pretty brunette."

7. It has been estimated that prior to the enactment by Congress of the Tax Equity and Fiscal Responsibility Act (TEFRA) in 1982, 16 percent of tips went undeclared. A recent Internal Revenue Service report concludes that the only form of income less likely to be reported was illegal income, with a 5 percent compliance rate (Citron 1989:9).

8. This article is also interesting in that it provides a vivid illustration of how the customer/writer perceives his relationship to the server, that is, as one who issues commandments to another, or more candidly, as supreme power to humble servant.

Chapter 3. The Limits of Managerial Authority

1. *Authority* is used here in its conventional sense to mean both the power and the right to issue orders, take action, gain compliance (*Webster's New World Dictionary*, 2d ed., s.v. "authority"). While it is recognized that power is not predicated on authority (Lamphere 1974:99), they are mutually implicated in the case of both the foreman and the manager, in the sense that loss of one entails loss of the other.

2. When a new manager challenged this fiction and insisted on fulfilling a customer's request for a milk

shake, a high-ranking waitress whizzed her order book at him and threatened to cut all the customers' tires. A possible explanation for the intensity of the waitress's response is presented in Chapter 4.

3. One waitress, a born-again Christian, extended her expectations of tangible payment for service rendered to her dealings with God. In a taped interview she recounted two occasions on which she had lent money: once to a hostess who claimed to be broke; once to a stranger who claimed to need money to get his family home. The waitress discovered she had been duped in both cases. A $20-bill fell from the hostess's pocket immediately after she had pocketed the waitress's loan of $10, and the stranger never fulfilled his promise to send back $20 when he and his family arrived home. Nevertheless, the waitress felt she had been repaid for her good deeds.

> I never saw the money again . . . but I knew in my heart that because I took a step of faith . . . the Lord would take care of it. I can't tell you how many things worked out to my benefit after that. And I can see God's hand in it. . . . I got $120 packet worth of [school] pictures for free. . . . My mother-in-law bought me a microwave cart right after that for my birthday. . . . We found it for $20 less than it had been, and then it went on sale and they gave us another $20 . . . and what else? I had had dishes on layaway and then I saw an ad in the paper and they were more [like] the ones I wanted. . . . So I . . . canceled the layaway and went back . . . to buy the other dishes . . . and they were even less than what they were on for the sale price. . . . *So it's just so many ways I think that God provides when you're willing to do for others.* (emphasis added)

---

4. The positive construction of responsibility may be promoted by higher-order management and management strategists as a means of motivating employees to assume additional duties and obligations voluntarily (Kay Warren, pers. com. 1989). As we shall see, this motivating strategy is unsuccessful in the restaurant.

5. *Pulling bus pans:* carrying full bus pans from the floor and kitchen to the dish room.

6. *The line:* area in which cooks prepare orders. Generally speaking, a long, narrow, and compact kitchen, partitioned off from the rest of the back house (see also Chapter 6).

7. *Drop:* put in the deep fryer to cook.

8. *Work off the floor:* finish up with parties in progress and clean and reset all tables. When possible, a waitress starts to work off the floor toward the end of her shift so that she can leave work on time.

9. This informant was actually a public accountant who moonlighted at the restaurant. Though he did not formally hold the title, he is referred to in this work as a manager, because it was in this capacity that he most often functioned, and because he was regarded as a manager—albeit an exceptionally hardworking and popular one—by managers and employees alike.

Chapter 4. Sources of Autonomy

1. *Low-a-lator:* deep, circular well in countertop in which plates, saucers, or bowls are kept. By pushing down on the stack, the server activates a spring mechanism that pushes plates from below the level of the counter up within reach.

2. Sufficient supplies are crucial to the waitress's ability to serve her customers efficiently, yet shortages

are and apparently always have been a constant of restaurant work. Donovan (1920:41) describes waitresses stacking dirty glasses on a shelf "where they could be grabbed and used again." Mars and Nicod (1984:40–42) report that waiters in English hotels reuse unwashed dishes, spit-clean cutlery, and stockpile supplies behind curtains and on the floor under side tables to ensure they will have sufficient stock for their own customers when supplies start to run low.

3. *Prices:* writes the price of each item in the appropriate space on the check.

4. *Cooks' window:* large opening in the partition between the line and the waitresses' station. In some restaurants, the cooks' window opens directly onto the floor, or faces the customers' counter. Orders that are ready to be delivered are placed on the wide sill of the window (the *pass bar*) and are said to be *in the window* or *up*. Most waitress–cook communication takes place through the cooks' window.

Wheel: circular, metal band suspended in the cooks' window. Waitresses clip checks to be cooked onto the wheel to the right of checks put in earlier, then spin the wheel so that the checks face the cook. This system ensures that orders will be cooked in the order that they are put in.

5. *Two-tops:* tables for two. Also referred to as *deuces*. Tables for four are referred to as *four-tops*.

6. Seniority, not age, is the basis for establishing authority at Route—and the two do not necessarily coincide. The speaker quoted here is in her midtwenties, and still younger waitresses hold high seniority and wield considerable power in the restaurant. Conversely, some older waitresses with little experience exercise minimal influence. Seniority and absolute age of employee may correspond more closely in older units (Kendelport was

only ten years old) or in restaurants in which turnover is less severe.

7. There is a striking similarity here to the Malay reapers and threshers described by Scott (1985:259), who solicit higher wages and piece-rates for poor conditions (for example, an especially wet or immature paddy) by grumbling loudly over the difficulty of the work, and lamenting the money they are losing, thereby signaling to the farmer "that he is in danger of losing his work force." Whereas the waitress frequently makes her ultimatums explicit, reapers and threshers rarely express their threats or demands directly. This difference suggests that the power differential between manager and waitress is less than that between Malay farmer and laborer, for "the greater the disparity in power between the two parties [in an encounter], the greater the proportion of the full transcript that is likely to be concealed" (Scott 1985:286).

8. The president of Red Lobster maintains that the company wants to "remove the spiel and inject the personality" in the service encounter. His choice of imagery suggests that the process of personalization will be controlled by the company, not the server; that the company will prescribe the dosage and brand of personality to be "injected."

9. Rationalization also increases the interchangeability of workers and decreases employee training time, and may therefore be a response to high turnover rates in the food service industry. To the extent that rationalization engenders tedium, eliminates meaning and challenge from work, and facilitates movement between jobs by removing the need for experience, it is likely to exacerbate the problem it is intended to relieve.

10. Carl Jerome (n.d.) contends that "dirty or

unpressed uniforms are a sure sign of an uncaring, unprofessional server." In fact the reverse is often the case, since the server who works hardest and most quickly tends to get the dirtiest. There is, moreover, a chronic shortage of uniforms in many restaurants, and a waitress is often compelled to wear the same grease-stained, fudge-splattered, sweat-soaked polyester apron several days in a row, much to her personal vexation.

11. Blackman's suggestion that donning a uniform is an act of subordination supports Goffman's (1971: 40–41) observation that individuals of lesser status have smaller "territories of the self" and exercise less control across territorial boundaries.

Chapter 5. Up a Crooked Ladder

1. Spatial mobility, which occurs through migration or work-related travel and relocation (Caplow 1954: 60–61), is not considered as a separate category here.

2. Restaurant cooks received a score of 16, waiters a score of 10 on the National Opinion Research Center (NORC) prestige rating scale. By contrast, college professors scored 93; janitors, 8 (Montagna 1977:32–35).

3. This is largely due to the precision needed to cook breakfast foods, which are easily under- or overdone and lose heat quickly. A strong breakfast cook must also be able to "cook eggs," that is, turn over-easy and over-medium eggs quickly without breaking the yolks. This is a crucial but rare skill, even among experienced cooks.

4. A similar pattern of horizontal mobility with an emphasis on the quality of interpersonal work relationships was observed by Howard Becker (1952) among public schoolteachers.

5. However, by leaving the company she will lose her profit-sharing option and her insurance, if she is covered by Route.

6. Hostesses usually become waitresses, and dishwashers sometimes become cooks.

7. This view is expressed especially clearly in Matina Horner's (1972) fear-of-success argument. An argument could be made that competitiveness is not a quality to be desired and that the concept of deficient competitive drive is therefore unsound. Lois Hoffman (1972:150) concludes her analysis of the development of women's achievement motives with the observation that the predominantly male ability "to suppress other aspects of the situation in striving for mastery is not necessarily a prerequisite for mental health or a healthy society. . . . A richer life may be available to women because they do not single-mindedly pursue academic or professional goals." For the most part, however, this tone of skepticism is lacking in the literature on women, and the male pattern of aggressive competitiveness remains the implicit ideal.

8. As managers were not asked to disclose their salaries during interviews, exact figures for management earnings are not available. One manager remarked that college students think they are going to make $35,000 a year as managers, and added, "To be honest, we don't get that kind of money." He went on to comment that when *he* finished school, "To get $20,000 to work in a restaurant, that was excellent," and emphasized that he "started out well below that." From these comments it might be inferred that managers at Route begin at an annual salary of around $20,000. The general manager reported that a strong, full-time waitress can make approximately $400 a week take-home, and Nera, the waitress known for making the best tips, claimed, "Right

now, the lowest amount that I'm making . . . is $500 a week. . . . Even with the snow on the ground [snow slows business], [19]88, . . . I did $25,000." If the lower ($400 a week) figure is taken for the waitress's income, and two weeks are subtracted from her earnings, since she receives no tips during her vacation (if she takes one), then the annual incomes of waitress and manager are roughly equivalent. However, the waitress makes $10 an hour for a 40-hour week, while a manager working a 70-hour week receives an actual hourly wage of $5.50.

9. This demotion was usually discussed as fact rather than rumor by employees. The manager himself did not mention the demotion in recounting his work history.

10. Because it took place after research ended, information concerning the cause of the demotion was difficult to obtain. It was rumored by some that the district manager had voluntarily abdicated his position because he was tired of the strain, but this may have been a face-saving explanation put out by the company.

Chapter 6. Resisting the Symbolism of Service

1. Though servants are still employed in some households, domestic service is referred to here in the past tense because it is no longer a commonplace of middle- and upper-middle-class life, as it was in the last century.

2. Hortense Powdermaker (1939:48) notes that in the deep South, whites lock the back door against thieves when they leave the house, but leave the front door open on the assumption that "no colored person would go in the front way and, apparently, that no white person would steal." This gives some indication of how

seriously conventions of interaction may be taken by the superordinate class or caste.

3. Factory dress codes may also serve to diminish the employee's status, but hard hats and protective goggles are more easily justified on practical grounds than chef's hats or blue eye shadow for female flight attendants.

4. Hochschild (1983:178) reports that the management of one airline "objected to a union request that men be allowed to wear short-sleeved shirts on warm days, arguing that such shirts 'lacked authority.'" John Molloy (1977:50) contends that long sleeves are essential to the standard "success suit."

5. The uniform of the female executive serves additionally to conceal her femininity. Molloy (1977:50) recommends that women wear "man-tailored" jackets, cut to "cover the contours of the bust," and man-tailored shirts as well as carry attaché cases. A full-blown "imitation man look" (complete with pinstriped suit and tie) is discouraged on the grounds that "when a woman wears certain clothes with male colors or patterns, her femaleness is accentuated" (1977:28).

6. Goffman's (1971:38–40) "information preserve" roughly corresponds to Georg Simmel's (1950: 322–24) notion of "intellectual private-property." Both encompass biographical facts about the individual, in which category first names may be included. As in the case of dress codes, the server's formal lack of control over the borders of this territory of self reflects her low status.

7. For current examples see "Service with a Sneer" (Lanpher 1988), "Getting Serious about Service" (Barron 1989), "Sure Ways to Annoy Consumers" (Wessel 1989), "Guerrilla Tactics for Shoppers" (Franzmeier 1987), and "Friendly Waiters and Other Annoyances"

(Burros 1989). A common motif in service articles, and one which is commonly portrayed in the accompanying illustrations, is the service worker who eats, reads, or watches television while a long line of customers gathers cobwebs, grows old, or undergoes bodily decay while waiting to be served. In his examination of factors that contribute to the anxiety of waiting, David Maister (1985) suggests that the sight of service workers not serving while customers wait in line is irritating, because to the customer, the wait is "unexplained." He remarks that "the explanation that the 'idle' personnel are taking a break or performing other tasks is frequently less than acceptable," but does not indicate why this should be the case. In light of the argument presented here, it might be hypothesized that customers become anxious or angry at least partly because the server's behavior challenges their perception of service as an encounter between master and servant. By subordinating the customer's needs to her own need or right (if on break) to drink, eat, or rest, the server violates the customer's self-image as master whose needs are by definition paramount. Further, by openly engaging in such blatantly human acts as eating, the worker flaunts her personhood and her equality to those accustomed to looking upon those who serve as nonpersons or as beings of a lower order.

8. Harris's failure to distinguish direct service from other forms of service work leads him to confuse emotions springing from opposed sources. The anger felt toward waitresses and bus drivers is akin to the sentiments of master toward servant; the anger and distrust felt toward doctors and government officials more closely resemble the feelings of servant toward master. While the former reflects impatience with the supposed mental and moral deficiencies of the powerless, the latter stems from the belief that money, knowledge, and authority are

being misused by those in power. One is the anxiety of the oppressor, the other of the oppressed.

9. It could be argued that the soldier is no more than a pawn of high-order military strategists. Still, soldiers are armed and commissioned to fight, rather than passively absorb the aggressions of enemy forces. Though they may be formally powerless, they wield power; though their actions are dictated from above, they are active.

10. *Take the cash* (usually *take cash*): ring up a check, take the customer's payment, and return the appropriate change. Many waitresses do not see this as part of their job, in part because there is a separate job code for hostessing (and hostess wages are higher than waitress wages), and partly because they frequently do not have time to spare from taking orders and serving food to assume register duties. For both reasons, waitresses often ignore customers waiting to pay at the register. Some waitresses take cash only for their own customers and some only for those of their customers who are paying by credit card or have not yet left a tip. In these cases the waitress is motivated by the possibility that a customer who has to wait to pay may become annoyed and fail to add a tip to the credit charge, or neglect to return to the table with a gratuity before leaving the restaurant.

11. Table allocation can be complex, since stations expand and contract depending on the number and strength of servers on the floor. The flexibility of station borders is incompatible with the servers' territoriality, and much of the confusion—and tension—concerning the distribution of booths and tables arises during station shifts, when the arrival or departure of waitresses and call-outs necessitate the reapportionment of tables, or require certain waitresses to *move up* or *over* to a new station.

12. It is improbable that this waitress actually anticipated losing her job as a result of her actions. Following the episode she went into the office and told her manager what had occurred. He told her, "Don't worry about it," to which she responded, "I'm not worrying about it. I'm just letting you know in case she [the angry customer] writes a letter to the main office." Apparently, the waitress thought it more likely that her manager would be questioned about the incident by his superiors than that she would be questioned by him. It is possible, but doubtful, that she feared top-down repercussions. Complaints received by unit managers from higher-ups are fairly rare and are typically passed on to the concerned waitress (particularly if she is competent) in softened form and an apologetic tone. In this case at any rate, "nothing ever came about" concerning the incident.

13. Riesman differs from Mills and Hochschild in identifying the source and purpose of personality manipulation. In Riesman's conception, the worker engages in false personalization or forced friendliness, not because it is his job to do so, but because personalization has been deemed desirable by his peers. In personalizing his work relations, the individual secures the peer approval that Riesman perceives as the central motivating concern of the other-directed character type of the twentieth century.

Chapter 7. Conclusion

1. If the working-class husbands in Rubin's study enjoyed the enclaves of autonomy discussed by Katz, their ration of control was presumably not sufficient to counterbalance their overall sense of powerlessness at work.

2. As one assembly-line worker described his job: "A car comes, I weld it; a car comes, I weld it; a car comes, I weld it" (Garson 1984:39).

3. This rejection of relativism is not inspired by the philosophy that in order to establish the equality of subordinate and dominant groups, or of self and other, it is necessary to prove the absence of difference. As Tzvetan Todorov (1984:42) points out, such a philosophy is no less egocentric than the belief that difference is intrinsically hierarchic. Both positions deny "the existence of a human substance truly other, something capable of being not merely an imperfect state of oneself." But if equality is not predicated on identity, difference is rarely absolute. Women and working-class men may have concerns that differ from, but are neither more nor less rational or worthy than, those of middle-class males. They will also have concerns in common. Among these may be counted an interest in receiving just compensation for their labor and a desire for autonomy.

References

Agar, Michael H.
>1980. *The Professional Stranger: An Informal Introduction to Ethnography.* New York: Academic Press.

Albrecht, Karl, and Ron Zemke.
>1985. *Service America!: Doing Business in the New Economy.* Homewood, Ill.: Dow Jones–Irwin.

American Anthropological Association.
>1983. *Professional Ethics: Statements and Procedures of the American Anthropological Association.* Washington, D.C.: American Anthropological Association.

Applebaum, Herbert, ed.
>1984. *Work in Market and Industrial Societies.* Albany: State University of New York Press.

Ardener, Shirley, ed.
>1975. *Perceiving Women.* New York: John Wiley, Halsted Press.

Bakke, E. Wight.
>1969. "The Worker's Job." In *The Unemployed Worker: A Study of the Task of Making a Liv-*

ing without a Job. Pp. 35–60. Hamden, Conn.:
Archon Books.

Barron, Cheryll Aimee.
1989. "Getting Serious about Service." *New York
Times Magazine.* June 11.

Becker, Howard S.
1952. "The Career of the Chicago Public School-
teacher." *American Journal of Sociology* 57(5):
470–77.

Blackman, Barry A.
1985. "Making a Service More Tangible Can
Make It More Manageable." In *The Service Encounter: Managing Employee/Customer Interaction in Service Businesses.* J. Czepiel, M. Solomon, and C. Suprenant, eds. Pp. 291–302.
Lexington, Mass.: D.C. Heath, Lexington
Books.

Blauner, Robert.
1969. "Work Satisfaction and Industrial Trends."
In *A Sociological Reader on Complex Organizations.* 2d ed. A. Etzioni, ed. Pp. 223–49. New
York: Holt, Rinehart, and Winston.

Braverman, Harry.
1974. *Labor and Monopoly Capital: The Degradation of Work in the Twentieth Century.* New
York: Monthly Review Press.

Burros, Marian.
1989. "Friendly Waiters and Other Annoyances."
New York Times. May 24.

Butler, Suellen, and James K. Skipper, Jr.
1980. "Waitressing, Vulnerability, and Job Autonomy: The Case of the Risky Tip." *Sociology of
Work and Occupations* 7(4):487–502.

Butler, Suellen, and William Snizek.
1976. "The Waitress–Diner Relationship: A Mul-

208

timethod Approach to the Study of Subordinate Influence." *Sociology of Work and Occupations* 3(2):209–22.

Caplow, Theodore.
1954. *The Sociology of Work*. Minneapolis: University of Minnesota Press.

Channon, Derek F.
1978. *The Service Industries: Strategy, Structure and Financial Performance*. New York: Holmes & Meier.

Chinoy, Ely.
1952. "The Tradition of Opportunity and the Aspirations of Automobile Workers." *American Journal of Sociology* 57(5):453–59.
1955. *Automobile Workers and the American Dream*. Garden City, N.Y.: Doubleday.

Citron, Zachary.
1989. "The Case against Tipping: Waiting for Nodough." *The New Republic*. January.

Davis, Fred.
1959. "The Cabdriver and His Fare: Facets of a Fleeting Relationship." *American Journal of Sociology* 65(2):158–65.

de Beauvoir, Simone.
1977. "The Existential Paralysis of Women." In *History of Ideas on Woman: A Source Book*. R. Agonito, ed. Pp. 343–60. New York: G.P. Putnam's Sons, Capricorn Books.

de Kadt, Maarten.
1984. "Insurance: A Clerical Work Factory." In *Work in Market and Industrial Societies*. H. Applebaum, ed. Pp. 74–87. Albany: State University of New York Press.

Donovan, Frances.
1920. *The Woman Who Waits*. Boston: Gorham Press.

Federbush, Marsha.
        1974. "The Sex Problems of School Math Books."
        In *And Jill Came Tumbling After: Sexism in
        American Education*. J. Stacey, S. Bereaud, and
        J. Daniels, eds. Pp. 178–84. New York: Dell.
Franzmeier, Stephen.
        1987. "Guerrilla Tactics for Shoppers." *Star* (Lantana, Fla.). August 25.
Fuchs, Victor R.
        1968. *The Service Economy*. New York: National
        Bureau of Economic Research.
        1985. "An Agenda for Research on the Service
        Sector." In *Managing the Service Economy: Prospects and Problems*. R. Inman, ed. Pp. 319–26.
        Cambridge: Cambridge University Press.
Garson, Barbara.
        1984. "Lordstown: Work in an American Auto
        Factory." In *Work in Market and Industrial Societies*. H. Applebaum, ed. Pp. 38–44. Albany:
        State University of New York Press.
Gershuny, J. I., and I. D. Miles.
        1983. *The New Service Economy: The Transformation of Employment in Industrial Societies*.
        New York: Praeger Publishers.
Gersuny, Carl, and William R. Rosengren.
        1973. *The Service Society*. Cambridge, Mass.:
        Schenkman Publishing Co.
Gifford, Courtney D., ed.
        1988. *Directory of U.S. Labor Organizations:
        1988–89 Edition*. Washington, D.C.: Bureau of
        National Affairs.
Goffman, Erving.
        1967. *Interaction Ritual: Essays on Face-to-Face
        Behavior*. New York: Pantheon Books.
        1971. "The Territories of the Self." In *Relations in*

Public: Microstudies of the Public Order. New York: Basic Books.

Green, Gordon W., Jr.
1989. *Getting Ahead at Work: A Proven System for Advancing at Work, Regardless of Your Occupation*. New York: Carol Communications.

Grogan, Bernard, head of research for the Hotel Employees' and Restaurant Employees' International Union (AFL–CIO).
1990. Telephone conversation with author. January 16.

Guest, Robert H.
1954. "Work Careers and Aspirations of Automobile Workers." *American Sociological Review* 19(2):155–63.

Harris, Marvin.
1981. *America Now: The Anthropology of a Changing Culture*. New York: Simon & Schuster.

Henderson, John P.
1965. *Labor Market Institutions and Wages in the Lodging Industry*. MSU Business Studies. Michigan: Bureau of Business and Economic Research, Michigan State University.

Hochschild, Arlie.
1983. *The Managed Heart: Commercialization of Human Feeling*. Berkeley: University of California Press.

Hoffman, Lois Wladis.
1972. "Early Childhood Experiences and Women's Achievement Motives." *Journal of Social Issues* 28(2):129–55.

Hollander, Stanley.
1985. "A Historical Perspective on the Service Encounter." In *The Service Encounter: Managing Employee/Customer Interaction in Service*

Businesses. J. Czepiel, M. Solomon, and C. Suprenant, eds. Pp. 49–63. Lexington, Mass.: D.C. Heath, Lexington Books.

Horner, Matina S.
1972. "Toward An Understanding of Achievement-Related Conflicts in Women." *Journal of Social Issues* 28(2):157–75.

Howe, Louise K.
1977. *Pink Collar Workers: Inside the World of Women's Work.* New York: Putnam.

Howe, Wayne J.
1987. "Strong Employment Growth Highlights First Half of 1987." *Monthly Labor Review* 110(9):64–69.

Jerome, Carl.
N.d. "Tips on Tipping: Ten Commandments for All Food Servers." N.p. (from newspaper clipping posted on Route bulletin board).

Josefowitz, Natasha.
1985. *You're the Boss! A Guide to Managing People with Understanding and Effectiveness.* New York: Warner Books.

Kanter, Rosabeth Moss.
1977. *Men and Women of the Corporation.* New York: Basic Books.

Karen, Robert L.
1962. "Some Factors Affecting Tipping Behavior." *Sociology and Social Research* 47(1):68–74.

Katz, Fred E.
1968. "Integrative and Adaptive Uses of Autonomy: Worker Autonomy in Factories." In *Autonomy and Organization: The Limits of Social Control.* New York: Random House.

Koepp, Stephen.
1987. "Pul-eeze! Will Somebody Help Me? Frus-

trated American Consumers Wonder Where the Service Went." *Time*. February 2.

Krause, Elliott A.
1971. *The Sociology of Occupations*. Boston: Little, Brown.

Kutscher, Ronald E.
1987. "Overview and Implications of the Projections to 2000." *Monthly Labor Review* 110(9):3–9.

Lamphere, Louise.
1974. "Strategies, Cooperation, and Conflict among Women in Domestic Groups." In *Woman, Culture, and Society*. M. Rosaldo and L. Lamphere, eds. Pp. 97–112. Stanford, Calif.: Stanford University Press.

Lanpher, Katherine.
1988. "Service with a Sneer." *Washington Post*. December 27.

Maister, David H.
1985. "The Psychology of Waiting Lines." In *The Service Encounter: Managing Employee/Customer Interaction in Service Businesses*. J. Czepiel, M. Solomon, and C. Suprenant, eds. Pp. 113–23. Lexington, Mass.: D.C. Heath, Lexington Books.

Malinowski, Bronislaw.
1922. *Argonauts of the Western Pacific*. New York: E. P. Dutton.

Mars, Gerald, and Michael Nicod.
1984. *The World of Waiters*. London: George Allen & Unwin.

Mauss, Marcel.
1925. *The Gift*. Glencoe, Ill.: Free Press.

McGill, Douglas C.
1989. "Why They Smile at Red Lobster." *New York Times*. April 23.

Mercure, Daniel, Daniel Regimbald, and Alain Tanguay.
1987. "Le Travail de Nuit Volontaire: Pour Preserver Son Autonomie." *Sociologie du Travail* 29(3):359–63.

Mills, C. Wright.
1956. *White Collar: The American Middle Classes.* New York: Oxford University Press.

Molloy, John T.
1977. *The Woman's Dress for Success Book.* New York: Warner Books.

Montagna, Paul D.
1977. *Occupations and Society: Toward a Sociology of the Labor Market.* New York: John Wiley.

Moore, Lynda L., ed.
1986. *Not as Far as You Think: The Realities of Working Women.* Lexington, Mass.: D.C. Heath, Lexington Books.

Morris, William, and Mary Morris.
1977. *Morris Dictionary of Word and Phrase Origins.* New York: Harper & Row.

Oxford English Dictionary, s.v. "tip," "gratuitous."

Parenti, Michael.
1978. "Interests and Consensus." In *Power and the Powerless.* Pp. 15–26. New York: St. Martin's Press.

Parnes, Herbert S.
1954. *Research on Labor Mobility: An Appraisal of Research Findings in the United States.* Bulletin 65. New York: Social Science Research Council.

Partridge, Eric.
1984. *A Dictionary of Slang and Unconventional English.* 8th ed., s.v. "stiff." New York: Macmillan.

Paules, Greta Foff.
1990a. "Behind the Lines: Strategies of Self-

Perception and Protection among Waitresses in New Jersey." Ph.D. diss., Princeton University.
1990b. "Up a Crooked Ladder: Conflicting Definitions of Responsibility and Advancement as a Problem in Organizational Culture." In *Cross-Cultural Management and Organizational Culture*. T. Hamada and A. Jordan, eds. Pp. 95–113. Studies in Third World Societies no. 42. Williamsburg, Va.: College of William and Mary.

Personick, Valerie A.
1987. "Industry Output and Employment through the End of the Century." *Monthly Labor Review* 110(9):30–45.

Phillips, S., A. Dunkin, J. B. Treece, and K. H. Hammonds.
1990. "King Customer: At Companies That Listen Hard and Respond Fast, Bottom Lines Thrive." *Business Week*. March 12.

Powdermaker, Hortense.
1939. *After Freedom: A Cultural Study in the Deep South*. New York: Viking Press.

Powell, Gary N.
1988. *Women and Men in Management*. Newbury Park, Calif.: Sage Publications.

Riesman, David, with Nathan Glazer and Reuel Denney.
1953. *The Lonely Crowd: A Study of the Changing American Character*. Garden City, N.Y.: Doubleday.

Rollins, Judith.
1985. *Between Women: Domestics and Their Employers*. Labor and Social Change Series. Philadelphia: Temple University Press.

Rothman, Robert A.
1987. "Direct-Service Work and Housework." In *Working: Sociological Perspectives*. Englewood Cliffs, N.J.: Prentice-Hall.

References

Rubin, Lillian Breslow.
>
1976. *Worlds of Pain: Life in the Working-Class Family*. New York: Basic Books.
Scott, James C.
1985. *Weapons of the Weak: Everyday Forms of Peasant Resistance*. New Haven, Conn.: Yale University Press.
Shostack, G. Lynn.
1985. "Planning the Service Encounter." In *The Service Encounter: Managing Employee/Customer Interaction in Service Businesses*. J. Czepiel, M. Solomon, and C. Suprenant, eds. Pp. 243–53. Lexington, Mass.: D.C. Heath, Lexington Books.
Simmel, Georg.
1950. "Types of Social Relationships by Degrees of Reciprocal Knowledge of Their Participants," and "Secrecy." In *The Sociology of Georg Simmel*. K. Wolff, ed. and trans. Pp. 317–44. New York: Free Press.
Spradley, James P., and Brenda J. Mann.
1975. *The Cocktail Waitress: Woman's Work in a Man's World*. New York: John Wiley.
Stanback, T., P. Bearse, T. Noyelle, and R. Karasek.
1981. *Services: The New Economy*. Totowa, N.J.: Allanheld, Osmun.
Stevenson, Richard W.
1989. "Watch out Macy's, Here Comes Nordstrom." *New York Times Magazine*. August 27.
Sutherland, Daniel E.
1981. *Americans and Their Servants: Domestic Service in the United States from 1800 to 1920*. Baton Rouge: Louisiana State University Press.
Todorov, Tzvetan.
1984. *The Conquest of America: The Question of*

References

troll

g at nee me

the Other. R. Howard, trans. New York: Harper & Row, Harper Torchbooks.

Turner, Victor.
1975. *Revelation and Divination in Ndembu Ritual.* Ithaca, N.Y.: Cornell University Press.

U.S. Department of Labor, Bureau of Labor Statistics.
1986. *Occupational Outlook Handbook.* 1986–87 ed. Bulletin 2250. Washington, D.C.: U.S. Department of Labor.

U.S. Department of Labor, Employment Standards Administration, Women's Bureau.
1975. *Handbook on Women Workers.* Bulletin 297. Washington, D.C.: U.S. Department of Labor.

Warren, Kay.
1989. Note to author. November.

Webster's New World Dictionary of the American Language, 2d ed., s.v. "authority."

Wentworth, Harold, and Stuart Berg Flexner, eds. and comps.
1975. *Dictionary of American Slang.* 2d supplemental ed., s.v. "stiff." New York: Thomas Y. Crowell Co.

Wessel, David.
1989. "Sure Ways to Annoy Consumers." *Wall Street Journal.* November 6.

West, James.
1945. *Plainville, U.S.A.* New York: Columbia University Press.

Whyte, William Foote.
1946. "When Workers and Customers Meet." In *Industry and Society.* W. Whyte, ed. Pp. 123–47. New York: McGraw-Hill.
1977. *Human Relations in the Restaurant Industry.* New York: Arno Press.

217

References

Whyte, William F., and Burleigh B. Gardner.
  1945. "The Position and Problems of the Foreman." *Applied Anthropology* 4(2):17–28.
Wolfson, Nessa, and Joan Manes.
  1980. "Don't 'Dear' Me!" In *Women and Language in Literature and Society*. R. Borker, N. Furman, and S. McConnell-Ginet, eds. Pp. 79–92. New York: Praeger Publishers.
Wray, Donald E.
  1949. "Marginal Men of Industry: The Foremen." *American Journal of Sociology* 54(4):298–301.

Index

Acting, deep, 160–61. *See also* Personality control

Advancement, 104, 106, 200n.6; in blue-collar settings, 49–50, 183–87 (*see also* Foremanship); employee views of, 60–62, 119–29, 175, 188; opportunities for, 117–18, 184; rejection of, 10, 49–50, 75, 117, 119–21, 129, 187; in white-collar settings, 13, 105–6, 188. *See also* Fill-in man; Managers

Agar, Michael H., 19–20

Airline industry, 100–101; dress codes in, 135, 202nn.3, 4; personality control in, 159, 160, 164

Albrecht, Karl, 17, 18, 100, 102

America Now, 139–40

Andy's Restaurant, 89, 94–95, 101–2; dress code at, 103

Ardener, Shirley, 165–66

Autonomy, 151, 205n.1, 206n.3; and advancement, 104, 124–27; emphasis on, 31, 32–33, 176–81 (*see also* Waitresses, and possessiveness; Waitresses, self-image as entrepreneur); sources of, 78–96, 145, 172–73; threats to, 96–99, 161. *See also* Noninterference, code of; Personality control; Rationalization

Bakke, E. Wight, 184, 185

Barron, Cheryll Aimee, 100, 140

Becker, Howard S., 199n.4

Blackman, Barry A., 102–3, 199n.11

Blauner, Robert, 177

Blue-collar workers, 53–54, 206n.2; and advancement, 49–50, 183–87; and auton-

219

Blue-collar workers (*cont.*)
omy, 177–78, 205n.1,
206n.3; dress codes for,
135, 202n.3; research on,
16–17, 18
Braverman, Harry, 53, 100,
170
Breaks, employee, 7, 29–30,
83–85, 202–3n.7
Busboys, 3. *See also* Dishwashers
Butler, Suellen, 24, 41–42

Cabdrivers, 23–24, 37, 41
Call-outs, 64, 123, 204n.11
Caplow, Theodore, 106–7,
199n.1
Centralization: in industry,
50–51, 53–54; in restau-
rants, 52–54, 65–66, 71–
72, 170. *See also* Rationalization; Routinization;
SPECs
Channon, Derek F., 17
Chaos, 13, 30, 169; as source
of autonomy, 80–83. *See
also* Supplies, shortages of
Chinoy, Ely, 50–51, 184–86
Citron, Zachary, 55, 194
Competitiveness: on day shift,
4, 28–30, 33; of women,
119, 200n.7. *See also* Tips,
strategies to increase
Cooks, 6, 63–64, 84, 86–87,
199n.3; compared to wait-
resses, 107–11, 199n.2; and
horizontal mobility, 112,
116; and quitting, 91, 93–

94, 96, 97; waitresses as,
112–16
Counterpart models, 165–66
Customers: on graveyard, 5–
6; possessiveness over,
146–47; as source of chaos,
82–83; typologies of, 24–
25, 35–36; waitresses' views
of, 12, 33–34, 152–53, 173,
193n.5. *See also* Personality
control, resisted by waitresses; Stiffing; Tipping;
Tips; Waitresses, custom-
ers'/public's view of; Waitresses, as servants

Davis, Fred, 23–24, 37
de Kadt, Maarten, 13
Dishwashers, 3, 6, 84, 87,
118, 134; and advancement,
200n.6; and managers, 109;
rank of, 107; turnover
among, 61. *See also* Fill-in
man
Domestics, nineteenth-
century. *See* Servants
Donovan, Frances, 44–45,
103, 193n.5, 196–97n.2
Dress codes, 78, 202n.5; and
rationalization, 102–4; status implications of, 134–36,
199n.11, 202nn.3, 4, 6; violations of, 81–82

Emotion control. *See* Personality control

False consciousness, 186

Federbush, Marsha, 135
Fill-in man, 13, 52, 60–65, 72–75, 104; and managerial turnover, 66–68; vulnerability of, 90–96, 123, 172–73. *See also* Management as prospective career; Managers
Foremanship, 50–52, 53–54, 190n.5, 194n.1; lack of interest in, 49–50, 183–87. *See also* Blue-collar workers
Fortune, 184
Fuchs, Victor R., 16, 17

Gardner, Burleigh B., 50, 51
Garson, Barbara, 206n.2
Gershuny, J. I., 16, 17, 18
Gersuny, Carl, 18
Goffman, Erving, 151, 160, 199n.11, 202n.6
Green, Gordon W., Jr., 60
Guest, Robert H., 183, 186

Harris, Marvin, 139–40, 203–4n.8
Henderson, John P., 54
Hochschild, Arlie, 13, 41, 100–101, 135, 159, 160, 161, 162, 163, 202n.4, 205n.13
Hoffman, Lois Wladis, 200n.7
Hollander, Stanley, 137
Horner, Matina S., 200n.7
Hostesses, 6, 107, 204n.10; and advancement, 200n.6; duties of, 3–4, 29, 62–63
Howe, Louise K., 39–40

Innes (Route manager), 66–67, 69–71

Jerome, Carl, 40–41, 100, 137, 198–99n.10

Kanter, Rosabeth Moss, 105–6, 107, 188
Karen, Robert L., 24, 41
Katz, Fred E., 78, 177, 205n.1
Koepp, Stephen, 17, 139, 140
Kula, 42–43
Kutscher, Ronald E., 16

Labor shortage, 2, 13, 69–70; and management, 60–62, 175; as source of autonomy, 81, 82, 95–96
Lamphere, Louise, 194n.1
Lonely Crowd, The, 161

Mae (Route waitress), 112–13, 114–16
Maister, David H., 202–3n.7
Malay workers, 198n.7
Malinowski, Bronislaw, 20, 42–43
Managed Heart, The, 160
Management, as prospective career, 60–62, 106, 119–27, 128–29, 175, 188. *See also* Fill-in man; Managers
Managers, 6, 145, 194n.1, 200–201n.8; and centralization, 52–54, 65–66, 170; disillusionment of, 66–69; and labor shortage, 60–62, 175; lack of respect for, 64–

Managers (*cont.*)
65, 74, 118, 127–28; levels
of, 4, 52, 111–12; status
anxiety among, 69–72; and
tipping system, 52, 54–59,
66, 84, 171–72; training of,
66–67, 70, 88; turnover
among, 66–68, 88–90, 106,
117. *See also* Advancement;
Fill-in man; Foremanship;
Quitting
Manes, Joan, 136
Mann, Brenda J., 25, 104
Mars, Gerald, 24–25, 26, 37,
42, 196–97n.2
Mauss, Marcel, 44
McGill, Douglas C., 100, 101,
102
Miles, I. D., 16, 17, 18
Mills, C. Wright, 50, 51–52,
158–59, 161, 205n.13
Mobility, 106–7, 199n.1; horizontal, 106–7, 112–17, 129,
199n.4; vertical (*see* Ad-
vancement)
Molloy, John T., 136, 202nn.4,
5
Montagna, Paul D., 7
Moore, Lynda L., 128
Morris, William, and Mary
Morris, 41–42

Nera (Route waitress), 38–39,
95, 97–98, 110, 179–81;
earnings of, 33, 200–201n.8
Nicod, Michael, 24–25, 26,
37, 42, 196–97n.2
Noninterference, code of, 27,

148–50, 175. *See also* Autonomy

Oxford English Dictionary,
42, 43

Parenti, Michael, 186
Parnes, Herbert S., 106
Paules, Greta Foff, 15, 182,
193n.4
Personality control, 158–61,
198n.8, 205n.13; resisted
by waitresses, 132, 150–58,
161–66
Personick, Valerie A., 16
Phillips, S., et al., 100
PICs, 4; vulnerability of, 123–
24
Powdermaker, Hortense, 201–
2n.2
Powell, Gary N., 128

Quitting, 74–75, 141; when
autonomy is threatened,
96–98, 177–78; as manip-
ulative ploy, 90–96, 172–73

Racial tension, 150, 193–94n.6
Rationalization, 82–83, 100–
104, 170, 198n.9; of
worker's interactive stance,
158–61, 163–64. *See also*
Autonomy, sources of; Cen-
tralization; Routinization;
SPECs
Red Lobster, 101, 198n.8
Relativism, 187, 206n.3
Research methods, 19–21; in-

terviews, 20–21, 190–91n.8, 192n.14

Resistance: "garden variety," 10, 181–82; silent, 164–66, 173–74

Responsibility, 196n.4; seen as liability, 60–62, 119–21, 123. *See also* Fill-in man

Restaurant industry: structure of, 12–15, 169–76; unionization in, 9–10, 52, 174–75, 190–91n.8, 191n.9

Riesman, David, 19, 161, 205n.13

Rollins, Judith, 44, 46

Rookies, 11–12, 27, 84, 118; managers as, 88–90; training of, 78–80

Rosengren, William R., 18

Rothman, Robert A., 7, 17–18, 134–35

Route, 2–7, 117, 189n.1, 197–98n.6; centralization at, 52–54, 71–72; compared to other restaurants, 14; occupational hierarchy of, 14, 52, 107–12. *See also* Shifts

Routinization, 53–54, 100–102, 175. *See also* Centralization; Rationalization; SPECs

Rubin, Lillian Breslow, 178, 205n.1

Scott, James C., 10, 142, 159–60, 164, 181, 198n.7

SCs, 4; vulnerability of, 123–24

Servants, 44, 46, 159, 201n.1; waitresses as, 8–9, 132–40, 160–62, 170, 173, 194n.8. *See also* Service

Service: criticism of workers in, 138–40, 202–3n.7 (*see also* Waitresses, customers'/public's view of); direct, 17, 18–19, 137–38, 162, 203–4n.8; "golden age" of, 140; rationalization of, 82–83, 100–104, 158–61, 170, 198n.9 (*see also* SPECs); sector, 15–19, 191n.10; symbolism of, 8–9, 132–38, 140, 163, 164, 170, 173 (*see also* Dress codes; Personality control; Tipping; Tips)

Shifts, 4, 8; and customer turnover, 189–90n.3; day, 4, 28–30, 32–33, 114; graveyard, 5–6, 29, 149; swing, 4, 29

Shostack, G. Lynn, 102

Sidework, 8, 59, 143–44

Simmel, Georg, 134, 202n.6

Skipper, James K., Jr., 41–42

Snizek, William, 24

SPECs, 77–79, 101; violations of, 80, 81, 88. *See also* Centralization; Rationalization; Routinization

Spradley, James P., 25, 104

Stations, 85, 190n.6, 204n.11; assignment of, 27, 88, 116–17; and possession, 146–48, 175

Stevenson, Richard W., 100
Stiffing, 5, 133, 165; wait-
    resses' interpretation of, 25,
    34–36; waitresses' response
    to, 12, 31–32, 35–36, 47,
    116. *See also* Tipping; Tips
Supplies, shortages of, 13,
    116, 196–97n.2, 198–
    99n.10; and creative prob-
    lem solving, 56, 81, 172
Sutherland, Daniel, 44, 133,
    134–35, 137, 138, 139, 140,
    159

"Ten Commandments for All
    Food Servers," 40–41
Terminology, restaurant, 4,
    33–34, 114, 141–42; *call-
    out*, 192n.1; *call out on*,
    123; *calls the wheel*, 87;
    cooks' window, 197n.4;
    drop, 196n.7; *the floor*,
    189n.2; *front/back house*,
    192–93n.2; *the line*, 141,
    196n.6; *low-a-lator*, 196n.1;
    pass bar, 197n.4; *pick up*,
    193n.3; *prices*, 197n.3;
    pulling bus pans, 196n.5;
    read codes, 113, 141;
    rushes, 7; *sat*, 29;
    stiff/stiffing, 35, 141,
    190n.4, 193n.5; *take cash*,
    204n.10; *thrown on the
    floor*, 80; *tip out*, 14; *turn-
    over*, 189–90n.3; *turn ta-
    bles*, 28; *two-tops*, 197n.5;
    up, 190n.7; *waitresses' sta-
    tion*, 141, 190n.6; *walkout*,

190n.4; *wheel*, 197n.4;
    work off the floor, 196n.8
Time, 139
Tipping, 13, 14, 145, 170; haz-
    ards of, 23–26, 47; incen-
    tive theory of, 55; and
    individualism, 174–75; and
    management, 52, 54–59,
    66, 84, 171–72; status im-
    plications of, 25–26, 41,
    44–46. *See also* Stiffing;
    Tips
Tips, 5, 39–40, 194n.7; and
    breaks, 84; earnings in, 33,
    47, 200–201n.8; and hori-
    zontal mobility, 116–17;
    server's interpretation of,
    25–26, 34–36, 38, 47, 173,
    193n.4; strategies to in-
    crease, 10, 12, 23–25, 26–
    33, 56–57, 171, 173–74;
    symbolism of, 40–46. *See
    also* Stiffing, Tipping
Todorov, Tzvetan, 206n.3
To-go orders, 8, 56, 145
Training: as cook, 109, 113–
    14; of managers, 66–67, 70,
    88; of waitresses, 78–80,
    172. *See also* Rookies
Turner, Victor, 41
Turnover, 116–17, 198n.9;
    among dishwashers, 61;
    among managers, 66–68,
    88–90, 106, 117; of tables,
    4, 28–29, 189–90n.3. *See
    also* Quitting

Unionization, 181–82; and

foremen, 50–52; in restaurant industry, 9–10, 52, 174–75, 190–91n.8, 191n.9

Waiters, 6, 117, 119; prestige rating of, 7, 107, 199n.2
Waitresses, 3, 197n.6; attitude changes in, 11–12, 152–53; and code of noninterference, 27, 148–50, 175; compared to cooks, 107–11, 199n.2; competitiveness of, 4, 28–30, 33; as cooks, 112–16; customers'/public's view of, 3, 103–4, 133, 138–40, 173, 194n.8, 202–3n.7; and horizontal mobility, 112–17, 129; income of, 5, 7, 33, 58, 79, 107; income of, compared to managers', 67, 122–23, 200–201n.8; job duties of, 7–8, 85–86, 114, 143–44, 170, 204n.10; and possessiveness, 31, 32, 143, 144, 145–48, 175; seen as destitute, 36–39, 46; self-image as entrepreneur, 140, 142–50, 158, 162, 166, 175; self-image as soldier, 140–42, 162, 166; self-images of, 10, 14; as servants, 8–9, 132–40, 160–62, 170, 173, 194n.8; training of, 78–80, 172; and unionization, 9–10, 174–75, 190–91n.8, 191n.9; views of customers of, 12, 33–34, 152–53, 173,

193n.5; working conditions for, 6–9. *See also* Advancement; Autonomy; Dress codes; Fill-in man, vulnerability of; Personality control; Quitting; Rationalization; Resistance; Service; Shifts; Stations; Stiffing; Tipping; Tips
Walking off the job. *See* Quitting
Warren, Kay, 196n.4
Watts (Route manager), 71–72, 73
Webster's New World Dictionary, 194n.1
West, James, 103
White-collar workers: and advancement, 13, 105–6, 188; dress codes for, 135, 136, 202n.5; and personality control, 158–59; in service industries, 17
Whyte, William Foote, 14, 25–26, 50, 51
Wolfson, Nessa, 136
Women, 128, 187, 188; and autonomy, 178–81, 206n.3; and competitiveness, 119, 200n.7; seen as passive, 15, 129, 163–64, 182; in service industries, 19; and silent resistance, 164–66; and tipping, 39, 170
Work and Occupations, 16
Wray, Donald E., 50, 51

Zemke, Ron, 17, 18, 100, 102